Praise for

Our Deepest Roots

"This book provides an overview of some of the impacts that traumatic experiences can have on relationships. Make no mistake, each of these topics—trauma and relationships—could fill a library. The power of *this* book is in the unique perspectives provided by the author. Dr. Towns is an experienced clinician with a focus on treating trauma and a member of the LGBTQIA+ community, familiar with the range of marginalizing, sensitizing interactions that permeate that experience. This alone could provide a powerful and important lens for an examination of these issues. But Dr. Towns brings us into her own life—her own marriage—in a very intimate and courageous way to show the reader how trauma, identity, early relational templates, and 'what happened to us' all play out in our most important loving relationships—in good ways and bad.

I highly recommend *Our Deepest Roots*. The key points can be generalized to fit non-LGBTQIA+ relationships and carry the key message that all relationships are fragile and fraught, yet full of hope and fulfillment."

— Bruce D. Perry, M.D., Ph.D.
Principal, The Neurosequential Network,
Author of "The Boy Who Was Raised as a Dog"
and "What Happened to You?"

"While I was reviewing this book, four words came to mind: insightful, compassionate, empathic, and deep. Dr. Towns has managed to capture the lived experience of trauma and present it back to the reader as if looking into a mirror. This will truly be a groundbreaking book in the field of trauma. It captures the queer experience and gives a new perspective to the existing heteronormative tools."

— Nick Erber, Ph.D., MA
Adjunct Counseling Professor

"As someone who has struggled with trauma and the impact it can have on relationships, I cannot recommend Dr. Jen Towns' book *Our Deepest Roots* enough. Dr. Towns provides a thorough and accessible guide to understanding how trauma can affect our relationships and offers valuable insights into navigating these challenges.

What sets this book apart is Dr. Towns' use of the Internal Family Systems Theory, which provides a framework for understanding how trauma responses develop and manifest in our interactions with others. Her writing is infused with both professional expertise and personal experiences, creating a powerful and relatable narrative.

One of the things I appreciated most about Dr. Towns' approach was her emphasis on creating a sense of psychological safety and authenticity. She consistently invites the reader to reflect on their own experiences and reactions, and provides space for processing and integration. I found this to be incredibly validating and empowering, as it allowed me to explore my own trauma in a supportive and non-judgmental way.

Overall, I highly recommend *Our Deepest Roots* to anyone who is navigating the complexities of trauma in their relationships. Dr. Towns' compassionate and insightful approach is a valuable resource for anyone seeking to build healthier and more fulfilling connections with themselves and others."

— Dina Proto, RN
Founder and CEO of Equality Healthcare Consulting,
Author of "Identity Impact"

"I found *Our Deepest Roots* to be a powerful look at how traumatic events shape our lives and how we can approach the healing process. Jen displays a startling and beautiful vulnerability by drawing from her own experiences. This makes for an incredibly authentic text about responses to traumatic events, a heartfelt examination of our 'parts'—that is, different pieces of our psyches—and how to view and react to particular events in our lives. At times, I found myself nodding in agreement, laughing with joy, or crying because I finally felt heard; the book feels life-affirming and soul-baringly real. This is someone who has lived with trauma and isn't just dispensing pablum to the masses; there is no feeling of 'take two therapy sessions and call me in the morning.' If you're feeling like something isn't quite right in your relationships, whether with yourself or with others, I highly recommend reading this book."

— David Rodgers
Professor, North Central Michigan College

"It is clear that Dr. Towns has an intuitive understanding of the transactional nature of trauma and how it affects relationships. In a time in the field of big name theorists coming forward with their own mental health struggles, Dr. Towns uses her own lived experiences with trauma tied together with tried and true methods and techniques from Attachment Theory, to produce this easy to understand and down to earth diamond of a resource for clinicians and non-clinicians alike. Her approach is practical, actionable, and most importantly, effective."

— Josh Smith, LMSW
Founder and CEO of DBT Institute of Michigan

"This book is long overdue. As Dr. Jen Towns so clearly describes, few members of the LGBTQIA+ community make it to adulthood without the burden of trauma. The challenges inherent in adult relationships can seem insurmountable. Dr. Towns is a gifted trauma therapist with a deep and personal understanding of the impact of such trauma on adult relationships. In a clear, coherent, and personal way, she provides a tool kit to help couples develop healthy and loving partnerships."

— Stacey Chipman, DHSc, LPC
Retired Clinical Director

Our *Deepest* Roots

Our
Deepest
Roots

NAVIGATING PAST TRAUMA
TO BUILD HEALTHIER
QUEER RELATIONSHIPS

Jen Towns, Ph.D., LMSW

PYP **Publish** Your Purpose

For permission requests, write to the publisher, addressed "Attention: Permissions Coordinator," at the address below.

Publish Your Purpose
141 Weston Street, #155
Hartford, CT, 06141

PYP **Publish** Your Purpose

The opinions expressed by the Author are not necessarily those held by Publish Your Purpose.

Ordering Information: Quantity sales and special discounts are available on quantity purchases by corporations, associations, and others. For details, contact the publisher at hello@publishyourpurpose.com.

Edited by: Nancy Graham-Tillman
Cover design by: Cornelia Murariu
Typeset by: Medlar Publishing Solutions Pvt Ltd., India

Printed in the United States of America.

ISBN: 979-8-88797-038-7 (hardcover)
ISBN: 979-8-88797-037-0 (paperback)
ISBN: 979-8-88797-039-4 (ebook)

Library of Congress Control Number: 2023903636

First edition, June 2023.

Publish Your Purpose is a hybrid publisher of non-fiction books. Our mission is to elevate the voices often excluded from traditional publishing. We intentionally seek out authors and storytellers with diverse backgrounds, life experiences, and unique perspectives to publish books that will make an impact in the world. Do you have a book idea you would like us to consider publishing? Please visit PublishYourPurpose.com for more information.

Dedication

"A tree lives on its roots. If you change the root, you change the tree. Culture lives in human beings. If you change the human heart, the culture will follow."
— Jane Hirshfield

For all the individuals who pick up this book—hear this—the past may inform the present, but does not have to predict the future. You can love. You can be loved. You can find happiness. You can redefine—everything.

For Brooke, without whom the big questions would have gone unasked—the deep roots, unearthed—the beautiful blossoms, unappreciated. Thank you for showing me how full life can be. I am the lucky one.

For my girls, may you always strive to discover and live in the truth of yourselves—individually and in love. May you grow to know and believe in your own strength and always pause to feel the warmth of the sun on your face.

Acknowledgements

To all those lovely souls who agreed to read through the multiple versions of this endeavor. You are appreciated beyond measure! To the PYP team, thank you for your steadfast encouragement. To my wife, for the hundreds of discussions over where to put commas or if I really needed to be *that* vulnerable. To my children, for the countless hours they put up with a computer on my lap.

Table of Contents

Foreword

I cannot stand it one more second. Every fiber of my being is telling me to run. Every muscle, every nerve, every bone. My skin is on fire with the need to get out. I stand up to walk out of the room and she escalates. Her voice grows louder, more pointed and shrill with each syllable. Her panic is palpable. The more I shut down, the worse she gets. I no longer hear what she is saying. Everything is white noise. My ears are ringing as I wander to the kitchen in search of my keys. *I have to get out. I have to get away. She has to stop talking. Please, God, make her stop talking. I will do anything to make her stop—stop speaking, stop needing things from me, stop following me around the house with her insistence. Just stop!* Her voice is like nails on a chalkboard, grating my nerves and scraping me from the inside out. I cannot fucking stand it.

I find my keys, grab my purse off the table, and look around for my shoes. *Where the hell are my shoes?* I grind my teeth as panic fills my chest, the weight of it crushing me. It is hard to breathe. She moves to stand in front of me, her lips moving and her hands gesturing—panicking. I cringe at the sound of her voice. The ringing in my ears is getting louder. I need her to stop talking!

Something inside me snaps and I start yelling, "I can't fucking do this! I have to get out! I'm done. We're fucking done!"

"Whatttt?!" she starts in, confused, then desperate. "What do you mean you're leaving? Where are you going to go? What am I supposed to tell the kids? Are you coming back? When are you coming back?"

She follows behind me as I collect my things. I don't care that her cries are turning to sobs right in front of me. I don't care that my words cut through her like a knife. I don't care that I am eviscerating the security we worked so hard to achieve. In this moment, I. Do. Not. Care. I slam the door behind me as I walk out to my car, but she catches it before it can close.

She holds it open and yells after me, pleading, sad, and angry. "You can't do this! You said you would never do this to me! Do you know how much you're hurting me right now? Hurting us? Do you even care?"

I stare at her, my mind blank. I have no response. I have no answers, no comfort to give. I need to get away. I will feel safe if I can just get away.

I open the car door and climb in. She's walking toward me now—one last attempt to keep me from leaving. It is too late. There's no turning back now. I need to go. I start my car and back out of the driveway. Ignoring her. Hurting her. I don't care. I put my car in drive and speed away.

I have not made it a mile when it hits me. The gravity of what just happened. What I said, what I have done to my wife—the person I love more than anything in this world—to our relationship—the first in which I have felt safe, held, and seen—and to myself—the fodder my inner critic will use against me for weeks.

She has called me three times already, all of which I have sent to voicemail. My phone lights up a fourth time. I stare at the phone with a lump in my throat. I pull over to the side of the road. Hands shaking, mouth dry, I answer the phone.

"Hi," I manage weakly.

"Hi," she replies timidly, unsure of what—or who—she will find on the other end.

Silence. Followed by more silence.

My mind races.

What am I supposed to say? There's nothing I can say! It's too late. This fuck up is far too big. I've ruined it all. Again. There's no point even trying to repair this. She hates me. She has every right to hate me. I ruined the best thing in my life. Why do I do this?

"Hello? Are you still there?" She momentarily snaps me out of my thought spiral and back into the present moment.

"I'm here," is all I manage.

Just apologize. Reassure her that you do not want to end this. Tell her how much she means to you. You can fix this; you at least have to try.

"Well, are you going to say anything?" she asks, her tone notably more clipped this time.

The silence continues.

*Well, why the hell is this all on me to say something? We wouldn't even be in this position if she had just left me alone and given me the space I asked for. It's not my fault. She pushed me to this point. I am entitled to space! What do **I** have to be sorry for?*

You left, that's what. You said you weren't going to leave again, and you left. You're allowed to be angry, you're allowed to need space, but you're not allowed to leave. You know the damage this causes. You know the way this plays on her anxiety and breaks her trust in you. This isn't new.

See, I told you. I fucked it all up—again. There's no point in saying anything. I said I wouldn't do something, and then I did it again anyway. I can never do anything right. I will always be broken. Healthy relationships are just not possible for me. I'm too damaged. I deserve to be alone. I think my parents were right, I'm just too hard to love.

You do not deserve to be alone! **We** *do not deserve to be alone! We have survived such hard things and, though we did not escape without many deep wounds, we are still deserving of love and forgiveness. We can do this. She deserves for us to be able to do this, and we deserve it too.*

Well, how is she supposed to know what she did wrong then? If I apologize, then she's going to think that I think this is all my fault, and it isn't! I refuse to accept all the blame. I told you I am done letting people walk all over me!

A car approaches from the opposite direction, and the beam from the headlights once again draws my attention back to the present moment. I look down at my phone and see that the call has dropped.

Oh, she hung up. Shit, she hung up!

I look both ways before whipping a U-turn and heading back in the direction of home. I see her sitting on the front steps as I pull into the driveway. Her head is bent and resting in her hands, her shoulders are slumped. She looks… defeated. She looks up as I close the car door, and I can tell she has been crying, ugly crying.

"Can I sit?" I ask, standing in front of her.

"Sure," she replies, without looking at me.

"I am really sorry," I begin. "I really do not want to leave. No part of me ever wanted to leave. I needed space, and those are not the same things. I never should have said what I said. I know I break your trust every time I say it, and I am really, really sorry."

She's quiet for a moment. She turns her head to look at me and I can see the sadness in her eyes, the hurt, the anxiety.

"It feels like every time I begin to feel secure in us again, you do this. You say things that make me question if you really want this. I know I want this; I am all in; I always have been. You're the one who keeps threatening to leave."

Her words hit like knives.

I hate that I am capable of making her feel like this. I hate hurting her this way.

The shame envelopes me like a thick, familiar blanket.

*Fuck this! I don't need this! Where is **her** culpability?*

I take deep breaths to quiet the defensiveness rising within.

We're just starting to get somewhere, and I will not add fuel to this fire again.

"I know," I manage in a whisper.

You need to go toward her. Reach out and hold her hand. I know it is hard. I know it feels so scary. You can do this. This is your wife. She is safe. This is safe.

I take a deep breath and place my hand on top of hers.

"I'm sorry my runaway part says and does things that make you question my commitment sometimes. I am not going anywhere, and I will not stop working with this part."

"I just love you so much, and I want to be able to trust you to stay, even when things get hard—especially when things get hard. And... I'm sorry too. I should've given you space when you asked for it. My angry part desperately wants to be heard and feels the need to repeat itself over and over again until you hear and understand my point of view. I know that's not helpful either."

Relief floods my whole system. I take a full breath for the first time in what feels like forever.

Maybe everything isn't ruined.

Of course it isn't.

Well, I still don't like that I had to apologize first, but it is nice that she said she was sorry too. I didn't expect that.

See, sometimes we have to give a little, or what may feel like a lot, in order to get what we need too. There are no villains here.

To some, this situation may sound like 17 different kinds of unhealthy, and in some ways, maybe it still is. To us, this sounds like progress. This sounds like hope. This sounds like healing. To us, being able to come back together and take responsibility for our own parts is monumental. To us, having a rupture like this be repaired in a matter of hours is extraordinary.

This did not happen overnight. It took years of therapy and thousands of conversations. And this level of fight does not happen daily anymore; in fact, it has not happened like this in years. But it used to. Now, she works hard to give me space and I work hard not to leave the house. She recognizes when she has a part that is insistently needing to be heard, and I try to hear her. I work hard at trusting that it is okay to love and be vulnerable, and she tries her best to show me that it really is.

To my younger parts, those who learned from the very beginning that connection is never to be trusted; to those who learned that people who claim to love you will most certainly hurt, abandon, and betray you; to those who learned that your value as a person comes from what you can do for others; and to those who learned that mistakes are intolerable and compassion is nonexistent—to all of those parts, this relationship feels like a gift. A gift that provides the space to learn from making mistakes. A gift that teaches accountability to acknowledge the effect my own behavior has on my partner. A gift that allows me to continue working to rewire my responses and correct my contribution to the negative cycle.

To folx who have never experienced attachment wounds, and to those who have not encountered interpersonal trauma, abandonment, or betrayal, I imagine this all sounds quite frightening. Thankfully, this book is not for them.

This book is for the folx who have been deeply wounded in their pasts and, despite their best efforts, continue to wound themselves and those they love most dearly. This book is for those who feel stuck in patterns of behavior that they cannot make sense of. This book is for those willing to do the hard, messy work of learning to love themselves authentically and, in so doing, learn to offer their partners the same love, compassion, and safety. It is not a road for the faint of heart, but from personal experience, I can tell you it *is* a road worth taking. Do it for your partner(s), do it for your relationship, but most importantly, do it for yourself.

— **Brooke Towns, LMSW**
Therapist, Queer Cisgendered Woman, Survivor, Wife

Letter to the Reader

Dear Beautiful Soul,

This book is about trauma. Not only is it about trauma we may have experienced in childhood or as adults, but it also interweaves the discussion about the inherently traumatic experience of being a part of the queer community in today's society. How could it not be traumatic? We are told on a regular basis either directly or indirectly that our "lifestyle" is "an abomination." We are told that we are "unnatural" and that we are going against greater plans of a higher being's intention. We live in constant fear of our marriages being dissolved with the flick of a pen or a raised hand that casts a vote. We are worried that helping the children of our community be their true, authentic selves may result in being investigated for child abuse or endangerment. As we walk down the street holding hands with our lovers, we are worried about what we might encounter. A leering glance? Some hateful words said under someone's breath in passing? An act of physical aggression or assault?

To be queer in today's society does not afford the peace of mind and body that some of our cisgender heterosexual counterparts experience. This is not to say that individuals who are cisgender or heterosexual do not have difficult lives; but rather that their lives are not made *more* difficult because of the added dimension of their sexual/affectual orientation, gender identity, or gender expression. Our relationships matter, and our identities provide unique relational aspects that cannot be addressed in a global manner.

As I was conceptualizing these chapters, I would often get the question of why I was writing this book or who specifically I wanted to market toward as the primary audience. Some individuals urged me to market toward a more global, mainstream society so that it could be applicable to everyone. However, so much of our lives are spent trying to carve out bits and pieces of information from the mainstream to apply to our queerness. Instead, I wanted to write something specific to the LGBTQIA+ population—where we get to be at the forefront. If this book, the topics therein, or any insight it provides can lend itself to the greater population, then I am glad for that as well. However, I wanted this to be a space where queer people are no longer square pegs forced into round holes.

As Chanté Adams so passionately said on stage at the Human Rights Campaign in 2022, "[This is] for every person that has ever lived outside the boring box of normalcy. You don't just deserve to be seen. You deserve to lead, to be the center of the storyline. You deserve the grace to make mistakes and be human. You deserve to be in spaces where you're the majority."[1] This book is for us. Please take

---

[1] Elizabeth Bibi, "Video and Photos: Vice President Kamala Harris, Actors Sheryl Lee Ralph, Abbi Jacobson and Chanté Adams Join Human Rights Campaign Incoming President Kelley Robinson at HRC Annual Dinner," Human Rights Campaign, October 30, 2022, https://www.hrc.org/press-releases/video-and-photos-vice-president-kamala-harris-actors-sheryl-lee-ralph-abbi-jacobson-and-chant%C3%A9-adams-join-human-rights-campaign-incoming-president-kelley-robinson-at-hrc-annual-dinner.

care of yourselves and each other as you navigate through this book and through this life that we all share.

Wishing you peace and connection,

Jen

Why Am I Writing This Book?

I have a history of trauma. It happened when I was an adult and has impacted my feelings about myself, my world, and my relationships ever since. It played on insecurities I had as a child and entrenched itself into deeply held negative beliefs about myself. As I navigated through graduate school and my work as a therapist for others, I started working on these beliefs in my own individual therapy. I became incredibly interested in the way our bodies and minds respond to trauma and are impacted after the fact. This prompted me to focus my professional work and continuing education on trauma-based interventions.

Then I fell in love.

I learned that my girlfriend at the time (who is also a trauma therapist) had a significant trauma history. Her experiences started when she was very young, and themes permeated throughout her development into her adult relationships and friendships. As we grew closer, the impact of our individual traumas started to bleed over into our relationship. We started fighting more:

She would get triggered by something I didn't know was a trigger.

I would get upset and defensive.

She would feel invalidated and pull away.

I would panic and try to "fix it" by overexplaining, lecturing, or blaming.

She would zone out, turn cold, push away, say hurtful things, or leave.

There would be explosions of raw emotion, words, tears, and defense mechanisms.

By the time the dust settled, we were left wondering what the hell just happened.

I would feel like a failure.

She would feel like a failure.

Loving each other was not enough.

We would *eventually* come back together, hug, apologize, and move forward. At first, this would take days or even weeks. Yes, she would come home if she left, but it might take hours before we spoke to one another and days before we touched. And any wrong move, perceived critique, or "dig" would light fire to an already tenuous and charged situation, which would then lead to further arguments.

Sooner or later, we would just get exhausted of being hurt and angry, life would keep moving forward, and the fight would get brushed under the rug. But these cycles would continue, and these fights would repeat. Even though both of us were in individual therapy, nothing was getting better or repaired long term in our relationship. Both of us felt increasingly guilty for hurting the other and frustrated because we were not getting our own needs met. We could individually work through some of our own triggers or responses, but together we would continue to trigger each other and cause more relational damage.

As we were considering what to do long term, we had to ask ourselves whether we could work things out. *Was it always going to be this hard? Should we stay together?*

I had been in relationships before that were toxic and abusive. This felt different. There was not a ramping-up cycle of violence, no totalitarian control, no jealousy, isolation, or manipulation. There was no intentional harm for the sake of dominance. Any behavior change I made was to help her not get triggered from her history of abuse, not because I was afraid or fearful of my safety. This *was* different. There was genuine love, support, and desire to repair. There was a mutuality. Fights actually seemed to start more internally, within ourselves than with each other, before they exploded outwardly. *Why was that?* We needed to learn more.

We started to do some real talking about patterns we were seeing in the clients we served (externalizing the issues sometimes helps take away some of the emotional charge that comes with personalizing the issues). We could see how our clients were interacting with their partners, their children, and their families. We could see the ripples of generational trauma, of queer identity trauma, and the differences between childhood and adult interpersonal trauma. Deciding to take some deeper dives into the literature and trainings, we researched the available options for both individual trauma treatment as well as treatment for couples. So many books read. So many trainings!

Ultimately, we were introduced to the concept of parts (different ego states or parts of ourselves that prompt reactions and are main players in the fights we were having). We started having more productive conversations about how attachment, parts, and triggers were impacting the way we took in and processed information. Instead of telling ourselves stories about what the other person was thinking, we started listening to each other. We started noticing patterns of interaction and identified some of the ways we were both trying so hard, but we were still not aligning in a way that was helpful to one another. We began having more conversations about intent versus impact in regard to relationships, and how our intent—to come closer and be more secure and safe—sometimes did not land the way we wanted it to, but rather came out in ways that had an opposite impact on our relationship. Combining all those elements, we started to talk more realistically about a model of treatment that integrated attachment, parts, the learned behaviors/beliefs from childhood, communication styles, and queer identity. Then we began testing it on our most convenient sample: ourselves.

Throughout this process, we got married, raised our children, and started our own business. We continue going to our own therapy (as all therapists should) and are constantly learning. We still fight—hard—and we continue to get triggered, say ridiculous things in anger, and threaten to sleep on the couch. But instead of leaving or threatening to end it all, we have learned ways to stay *and* feel safe, heard, and more together in the process of healing.

Having trauma is hard. Being in a relationship while you or your partner has a trauma history is hard. When both have a trauma history, it is *really fucking hard*. Trauma changes us—our sense of safety, our beliefs about ourselves and the world, and even our body chemistry. However, it *is* possible to have healthy and positive relationships that thrive despite the trauma. It is possible to develop compassion for your partner and other people so that you can better understand why and how they react. It is possible to reassure yourself and get your needs met while also holding space for your partner's feelings. Sacrifice of yourself, your partner, or your relationship is not required, but compassion, curiosity, and connection are. And you all already possess those things—they are what drew you together! Your curiosity about your partner's favorite food or most embarrassing moment, your deep and sensual connection, and your compassion for your partner's grief (such as when their loved one dies) is already baked into your relationship. You just have to use those skills in new (and sometimes fumbly) ways to rewrite old patterns and build new pathways to healing.

As with all stories, this is a perspective drawn from my reality, professional work, and personal experiences. This is *a* perspective, not *the* hard and fast rule. And this is *a* framework, not to be confused with any self-proclaimed *only* way to look at things. People are nuanced, and relationships are complicated. Take what you can from these pages and leave the rest. Some things will hit, others will miss, but I hope that you are able to resonate enough to find a few seeds of hope.

Understanding the Parts of Your Journey

You fell in love. You have a deeply visceral, sensual relationship and connection *and* you/they are hurting. *And* is a word that I will use throughout the book because it leaves room for the multiplicity of emotion. We can be in love *and* be hurting. We can care *and* be angry. We can want to dig into something so desperately *and* want to run in the other direction. We can honor the strength, resilience, and resourcefulness that we had to have to survive *and* recognize that some of those survival skills can impact our current relationships in tough ways.

This book is intended to help validate not only the multiplicity of emotion but the complexity of the *parts* we all have inherently within us. The idea of a parts-based psyche suggests that there are different facets of ourselves that may have different feelings about the same event (e.g., one part wants to call out of work while another part feels obligated to go in). We all have these different parts and use them throughout our day to fulfill a variety of roles. You may have a part that helps you be a dedicated and focused employee and another that allows you to be a silly and playful parent. You may have a part of yourself that is an incredible advocate or fighter, which helped you transcend through terrible experiences in your past and kept making you get out of bed in the morning. But this part may also be the first line of defense when you feel scared, attacked, or vulnerable, making you defensive when your partner asks if you remembered to pay the electric bill, is critical or harsh about dinner, or is frustrated about your sex life.

These different parts and states of our selves have fulfilled many roles and several purposes and brought us to where we are today. They can help us, *and* sometimes they can create a bit of chaos. They do not have a timeline or know that you are not in danger anymore, and they may be stuck in the past and are simply reacting in ways that keep you safe from any perceived threat. Trauma-based part responses are those big feelings that come from "somewhere else" deep inside. They are the "overreactions" we feel, such as disproportionate anger, horrible separation anxiety, and hyper/hyposexual drives. They are that voice that says, "I don't want to listen!"

Together, we will examine how these parts and states intertwine, how they influence our daily functioning, and how they impact our relationships with those around us. All parts are welcome here because they all serve a purpose, and their contribution to our existence is important (even if they have wreaked some serious havoc!). We enter into relationships not as a clean slate, but as an amalgamation of feelings, experiences, and passions. The goal of this journey is not to dispel or get rid of all those unique pieces of you, but to honor the roles they have played, see how they might currently be interacting with your world, and allow your adult self to take back some control. We must open that inner door, pull back the curtain, and dive into understanding why and how our past impacts our present.

Gaining insight about yourself will help you have a better understanding of and more compassion for your partner. This compassion and understanding are the cornerstones of any relationship, especially one that has a history of trauma. Sometimes all we need is a little guidance—a key to the map, so to speak—to point us in the right direction and catalyze a foothold upon which we can push our convictions forward. Hopefully this book will be that map, be that key, and put you on that path toward enhanced communication, compassion for one another and yourself, and a deeper connection than you thought possible.

How to Use This Book

This book is broken down into chapters that build upon one another in both content and relational development. We will begin with the most basic definitions of trauma and end with the intricate balance of relationship dances that involve infinite options of reaction and response. Each chapter includes examples that interweave key components of this book's model. The vignettes and case studies are based on fact, but some details and all identities were changed to respect privacy and confidentiality.

Throughout each chapter is also a combination of "takeaways," options for "deeper dives," and/or activities that will help you apply the chapter concepts to your situation. There is also a companion workbook that includes main concepts, questions/prompts, exercises, and additional activities that will help you dive deeper into applying these concepts to your personal life.

This book is not meant to be a replacement for individual therapy or relationship counseling. However, throughout the book are prompts to check in with your feelings, opportunities to take breaks if needed, and support given alongside the difficult topics we discuss. These check-ins will appear like the one below:

> Do a brief check-in with your parts and feelings. Do you feel anxiety anywhere in your body? Do you feel tightness in your chest, throat, or stomach? Take a small pause and look around the room you are sitting in. Take some long, deep breaths. Name five things you can see that are green. Name four things that are blue. Name three things you can reach out and touch. Name two things you can smell. Name one thing that is yellow. Take another deep and cleansing breath. Feel the weight of your feet on the floor. Feel yourself grounded in the here and now. If you feel a reduction in the tightness or anxiety and all your parts are comfortable continuing, please feel free to read on. If your parts are advocating for a break, please take one. This information will still be here, and you can come back at any time!

At times, we can get too caught up in the everyday stressors, and those little things become catalysts for big fights. However, not unloading the dishwasher is not usually the real root of the issue. The ideas in this book incorporate an upstream versus downstream ideology, because treating the downstream symptoms (e.g., communication, intimacy, daily interactions/tasks, money) of the bigger upstream issues (e.g., trauma, trust, safety) will only assuage the short-term outcome; you will find yourself repeating the same fights over and over again without solution or resolution. Getting to the root of interactions, attachment, trauma, and safety can assist in building a better awareness of how we process internal and external everyday information, as well as how our partners take in stimuli. And most importantly, it can show how those two realities interact to clash with or bolster one another.

Understanding the way we attach to others, the reasons for disruptions in that attachment, the intricacies of developmental trauma, the neurobiology of trauma, the multiplicity of ego states (how different parts of our psyche step in to protect us when we are feeling vulnerable), and the complexity of how trauma manifests into adulthood and relationships will give better insight into the balance between supporting our partners, supporting ourselves, and supporting our relationships. Along the way, we will dig deeper into defining these concepts and recognizing how they interweave into each person's individualized and beautifully deep roots.

Part 1

The "What?" of "My Stuff"

Chapter 1
Neurobiology of Trauma

If I want to grow and blossom as any tree would,
I have to start by knowing my roots
and understand how I came to be the tree I am.
– Jeffrey G. Duarte

"Because… trauma." That simple little phrase is anything but simple. It is a statement that provides an explanation for a wide variety of individual and relational issues.

- Why do I shut down or avoid my to-do list when I'm stressed? Because… trauma.
- Why do I get so angry when a plan or idea doesn't go as imagined? Because… trauma.
- Why do I sabotage relationships or find fault with every seemingly good person I date? Because… trauma.
- Why does it seem like even when my life is at its best, I still have waves of sadness or feelings that it can't be trusted? Because… trauma.

- Why, even in moments of great success or personal achievement, do I have a voice in my head that's inherently tearing me down or critical of my success? Because... trauma.
- Why, even after a fabulous sexual encounter, do I feel waves of depression or shame or reject my partner? Because... trauma.
- Why does holding my partner's hand in a movie theater bring waves of anxiety and disconnection even though I'm proud of my queer relationship? Because... trauma.
- Why do I cringe or roll my eyes when I hear the word "vulnerability"? Because... trauma.
- Why do I have (at least) two reactions to most things: what I believe I "should" feel/think and what I actually do? Because... trauma.

Trauma explains connection to seemingly unexplainable or unrelated issues, such as sex and depression, success and crushing criticism, and relational connection and unfounded suspicion. Some people might understand why they are reacting in a big way and others might not. Some might even see emotionless reactions or a take-charge attitude as character success and a positive attribute. There is not one singular definition of trauma among professionals, but the one thread that seems to pervade various philosophies is the idea that trauma can be both an event and the fallout of the event. We cannot discuss one without the other.

What constitutes something as being "traumatic" or having lasting effects is the idea that *it exceeds our internal ability to cope.* Humans have an amazing ability to adapt and survive; however, threats are not intended to be relentless. Our bodies and brains are not supposed to be consistently flooded with adrenaline or cortisol, making our hearts beat wildly, our breathing erratic, and our brains dissociate because pain is imminent. But when a child grows up in an unsafe or abusive atmosphere with a parent or caregiver, or when a partner is violent, that is exactly what happens. If the atmosphere is more than environmental—if it is also *relational*—the impact that it has on our internal psyche and the internalization of our sense of self is even more significantly affected.

As human beings, we are inherently programmed for connection, and we rely on our family of origin or caregivers for that connection. Connection assists in our ability to learn the language of our world. When our caregivers protect, nurture, and react to our distress consistently, we learn that we can rely on others to help us regulate. Depending on how they respond, we learn what is safe and how to manage internal distress, process relational stress, and navigate environmental factors. The effects of early traumatic events, and the healing thereafter, can have different outcomes depending on the level of support, consistency, and connection of a child's caregivers. This is one of the most impactful factors that determines resiliency.

Resiliency is not just our ability to get up when we fall (this widely portrayed definition needs to be debunked!). Instead, it is our inherent belief that we have support around and within us to help reestablish safety when dysregulated. It is our learned conditioning that if something adverse happens, we have the internal and external resources to work through that event. And it is the rewiring of our nervous system so that we can respond to stress without overactivation, because we have learned that we have some semblance of positive connection to those in our environment, the ability to internally stabilize through that consistency and connection, and some control over the outcome.[2]

There is a relational component to resilience, and the healing is not something we can do on our own. Without supportive families

---

[2] Bruce D. Perry, *The Boy Who Was Raised as a Dog* (New York: Basic Books, 2017), 311–314.

of origin, consistent and predictable environments, and access to resources, our bodies and minds can become incredibly hyperaware of our surroundings in order to eliminate the potential impact of stressful, scary, or dangerous situations. We switch into an automatic hypervigilance that is singularly programmed to keep us alive. If these dangers happen consistently, neural pathways develop that make our reaction times shorter and shorter so that our hypervigilance and awareness of potential threats becomes our new automatic response. The vignette below describes Jessie and his development of these trauma responses:

Example:

As far back as Jessie can remember, his father had an issue with alcohol. He would frequently come home intoxicated and would often hit Jessie's mother in front of him. When Jessie was three, his mother taught him that the sound of his father's truck in the driveway meant that he should hide under the bed and not come out of his room for any reason. The crunching of his father's work boots on the gravel driveway would make Jessie's heart race and his body sweat. He would hide in his room until the screaming stopped.

When he was 10, Jesse stopped hiding in his room and instead would try to protect his mother, often getting abused, either instead of or in addition to his mother. Jessie's mother would not step in to prevent his father from hurting him. Instead, she would tell him to "be quiet," "just do what he says," or to "try not to make him mad."

At 18, Jessie moved out of the house, went to college, and earned a degree in public relations. He has since been in several relationships, but his partners commonly claim that he varies between "cold and mechanical" and "closed off" or state that he "lacks passion." At work, Jessie has been passed over for promotions several times. He does not speak up in meetings and gets incredibly uncomfortable when he is asked his opinion about new marketing or strategies. He gets his work done days before it is due and tries to "stay under the radar" as much as possible.

Jessie is still operating as if he were 10 years old. He was conditioned from a very young age that certain sights, sounds, and smells equate to pain, fear, and lack of safety. Therefore, he is constantly trying to eliminate the possibility of conflict. He does not trust that his partners will protect him, his feelings, or his emotional wellbeing. Because he was taught that powerful men have the power to hurt, he is trying to remove all obstacles that might cause conflict. Jessie is operating in the present as he *had* to operate in the past.

When we transition out of a scary environment and into seemingly benign situations, the story we tell ourselves about every intention, motivation, or situation has a nefarious flair because of our internal narrative that our environment is scary. Just like Jessie, we are suspicious of our surroundings, guarded against developing relationships, and programmed for survival. Unfortunately, while this may keep us safe, it does not allow us to experience connection or a full range of emotion (including all the positive ones) since we are focused only on survival. Our map apps have not been upgraded; we are operating with an old Yahoo maps printout from 1996. Roads have closed, turns have changed, and one-way streets and roundabouts have been developed. All this creates incredibly difficult navigation in our present day. We expect roads to be full of bumpy gravel potholes and are bracing ourselves accordingly—even if the road is newly paved.

Having a better understanding of why these trauma-based responses are connected and how we can navigate through them can lead to increased empathy and compassion. And compassion allows for greater connection to our selves, our partners, and our relationships.

Brain Structure

The human brain is a beautiful structure, and its reactions to threats are primal. These reactions are deeply ingrained responses that an individual does not *think* through but instead *responds* to based on external stimuli. If you are walking down a dark alley, for example, and someone starts following you, your brain tells you that the situation is unsafe by going through a series of chemical responses that indicate to your body that it needs to respond. This activation turns off the rational thinking part of your brain (the prefrontal cortex) because it knows you will not have time to think about the several possible responses and multiple rational options. Instead, it sends signals that increase your heart rate and send blood pumping to your extremities, readying you to freeze, run, or fight off the threat. Once you hurry through the alley, get to the street, and climb into a cab, your heart rate slows, your breathing normalizes, and you have access to all parts of your brain that will allow you to process the event. Your prefrontal cortex comes back online, and you can reassure yourself that you are safe, call a friend to talk about what just happened, and plan to take a new way home the next time.

However, continuous trauma can hijack responses meant to be short term and keep hitting the repeat button. The reason for this is the brain's number one goal in life: to stay alive. Therefore, the amygdala (a tiny almond-shaped structure in the hippocampus) scans the environment 200 times per minute to assess whether the environment you are in currently resembles any likeness to a scary, painful, or unsafe environment in the recesses of your memory.[3] If the brain senses danger, these sensory triggers then send a domino-effect response to other areas of the brain and body, connecting old trauma memories to the current scenario and activating your body's survival responses (e.g., rapid heart rate, pupil dilation, increase in blood pressure).

In survivors, the amygdala can become extra sensitive to potential threats, and it may also have a harder time being calmed once triggered.[4] This is one reason many survivors experience fight/flight/freeze reactions to things that bring up memories of their abuse, even when the situation appears safe to others. This reaction/response happens before they are conscious of the triggering event or situation; their body just responds. A veteran falls to the ground to "take cover" the moment the fireworks go off, not because they were consciously drawing the connection between the noise and the threat, but because their brain did that for them in a nanosecond.

Not only are there sensory triggers that can activate bodily responses, but there are also **emotional flashbacks** that can occur when the amygdala recognizes a **relational trigger**, something that feels like a scary experience, such as rejection, abandonment, or emotional neglect. These relational wounds are then connected to relational/emotional responses, or ego state/protector activation, which we will talk about more in the next chapter. Both sensory and emotional flashbacks are very common with complex post-traumatic

[3] Lisa M. Shin, Scott L. Rauch, and Roger K. Pitman, "Amygdala, Medial Prefrontal Cortex, and Hippocampal Function in PTSD," *Psychobiology of Posttraumatic Stress Disorder: A Decade of Progress* 1071, no. 1 (2006): 67–79, https://doi.org/10.1196/annals.1364.007.

[4] Luke Norman et al., "Attachment-Security Priming Attenuates Amygdala Activation to Social and Linguistic Threat," *Social Cognitive and Affective Neuroscience* 10, no. 6 (2015): 832–839, https://doi.org/10.1093/scan/nsu127.

stress disorder (CPTSD), which is a more complex response to trauma that is typically learned over the span of repeated trauma, including relational or interpersonal.

CPTSD

The causal factors that manifest the development of a post-traumatic disorder can separate post-traumatic stress disorder (PTSD) from CPTSD. While PTSD can occur when individuals experience many different types of trauma from such events as a car accident, natural disaster, or single interpersonal incident, CPTSD typically develops after repeated interpersonal trauma in which there is a factor of **totalitarian control**, or total oppressive control.[5] This control can be the result of an adult–child relationship (parent or otherwise) or any type of relationship in which there is a significant difference in the power dynamic. The presentation of symptoms in PTSD versus CPTSD differ as well. PTSD primarily consists of nightmares, flashbacks, hyperarousal and startle response, and bursts of emotion such as **affect dysregulation**.[6] CPTSD symptoms include all of those, plus a change of **self concept**. A person's self concept is how they see themselves, their perpetrator, their morals and values, and their feelings of safety and trust in the world, even their existential faith.[7] This can overhaul a survivor's entire worldview as they try to make sense of their trauma.[8] We can see this in individuals who

---

[5] Judith Herman, *Trauma and Recovery* (New York: Basic Books, 2015).

[6] American Psychiatric Association, DSM-5 Task Force, *Diagnostic and Statistical Manual (DSM-5)*, 5th ed., (New York: American Psychiatric Association, 2013): 271–272.

[7] Pete Walker, *Complex PTSD: From Surviving to Thriving: A Guide and Map for Recovering from Childhood Trauma* (Scotts Valley, CA: CreateSpace, 2014).

[8] Bruce D. Perry and Oprah Winfrey, *What Happened to You?: Conversations on Trauma, Resilience, and Healing* (New York: Flatiron Books, 2021).

develop negative cognitions (beliefs) that they "aren't good enough," "deserved or caused the trauma," and/or "don't deserve love," and those who have internal blueprints of what love really is and how it should be expressed. These cognitions often incorporate levels of guilt and shame that are attached to the trauma as well as internal beliefs about self-worth. For a full breakdown of PTSD versus CPTSD symptoms and causes, please see the appendix.

Example:

Susan learned through past trauma that if she altered her behavior in specific ways, her actions might control the moods of others, and she might get her needs met through that mood management or mitigation. In her past, her older brother would repeatedly yell at and hit her if their parents were not home. She discovered that if she made him a special snack as soon as her parent's left, he was less likely to hurt her and more likely to either leave her alone or treat her kindly. Thus, she learned that if she could control his moods through her actions, she could get her needs of safety met.

Fast forward to present day. Susan's partner Mia is supposed to be home at 5:00 p.m. for dinner. Susan prepared Mia's favorite meal because she knew Mia had a long day and wanted to make her feel appreciated and seen. Perhaps, however, there is a part of Susan that really needs connection, had a difficult day herself, and does not have the energy or ability to react to Mia's stress if she comes home and starts to unload. Susan has learned through her trauma experiences that she could mitigate that to a certain extent, so she makes Mia's favorite dinner. To the outside observer, this could be seen as doing something lovely for her partner. However,

> When individuals experience emotional flashbacks that are triggered by present-day relational dynamics, their interactions with their partners are played out through the eyes and words of a traumatized child.

there could be other motivations for this. Susan is already coming into the situation with an agenda: to get her own needs met by making Mia feel a certain way.

In any situation, we have to ask ourselves whether there is an expected outcome or agenda. In Susan's case, her agenda of getting her own needs met is inherently set up for failure. What if Mia does not respond as Susan expects? What if Mia is not hungry? What if Mia has a migraine and wants to go lie down? So many external factors exist within this plan! So, if Mia comes home and does not immediately respond the way Susan expects, there will likely be a toppling effect for Susan. She might end up feeling frustrated that her need for connection or appreciation was not met, which could lead to feelings of worthlessness, which could cause Susan to question the overall relationship dynamic. Susan is then likely to react from a place of rejection and frustration, resulting in her getting angry at an unaware Mia, possibly pushing Mia away emotionally, or even yelling at her. The spiral is real! In this situation, Susan is throwing a football downfield, expecting that Mia will know the play, have the energy to run downfield, and be there to catch it expertly. But no one clued Mia into that plan.

Figure 1. Susan and Mia's Parts Dance.

Figure 1 illustrates Susan's and Mia's trauma-response spiral:

- Susan learned to mitigate stress to get her needs met.
- Susan mitigates Mia's stress with her own agenda.
- Mia is unaware of Susan's agenda and does not respond the way Susan wants her to.
- Susan reacts as being rejected and shamed.
- Mia responds with anger.
- Susan becomes even more upset with Mia's response and feels more shame, guilt, and self-loathing.
- Mia is put in the position to respond by regulating Susan's stress.

When these trauma responses play out in our interpersonal relationships, it is helpful to ask ourselves who is responding. In doing this, we can more easily identify whether our calm, curious, adult self is responding to our partner—or if a trauma-led part of us is driving the bus. In chapter 5, we'll examine these "parts dances" more closely.

Window of Tolerance

The **window of tolerance** is the body and brain's window where access to the prefrontal cortex is still relatively available. It is where we can feel our feelings, connect to others, and still form rational thoughts.[9] Remember, the prefrontal cortex holds our ability to access rational thinking, including executive functioning, rational thinking, and calculation. When the body gets activated because of a trigger, it responds by going through a variety of mechanisms meant to provide it with enough energy to escape the situation. However, if we are unable to escape, or if our window of tolerance is too small (due to habitual activation), we will exceed our window and transition into fight, flight, freeze, or collapse. Once we are in these survival-mechanism states, we have minimal access to that rational processing area of the brain.

When we are born, we are preprogrammed with a pretty standard-sized window of tolerance (although there are emerging discussions of how generational trauma and epigenetics may play a role in the original size of your "window"). However, individuals who have experienced trauma and consistent body activation will have a smaller window of tolerance. This is because their body must activate and respond quickly to keep itself safe from potential danger. When our brains and bodies recognize the capacity for scary things happening, they begin to sensitize us to the possibility of

---

[9] Daniel J. Siegel, *The Developing Mind: How Relationships and the Brain Interact to Shape Who We Are*, 2nd ed. (New York: The Guilford Press, 2012).

those things happening again, thus decreasing the size of our window of tolerance and risking our becoming stuck in a state of being habitually "on" or "off."

Figure 2 illustrates the window of tolerance.[10] The dotted lines signify the standard-sized window, the flowing blue line shows a typical stress response of ebbing and flowing at a gentle rhythm, and the jagged red line shows the stress response of a person who has experienced habitual trauma. Since these individuals typically have a higher baseline level, they start higher toward the top of the window, indicating that they are primed for response or reaction. The abrupt ups and downs signify their body and brain responses to the traumatic event, which vary between extremes of hyper and hypoarousal and could lead to the real possibility of becoming "stuck on" or "stuck off" as the insidious or continued trauma is experienced.

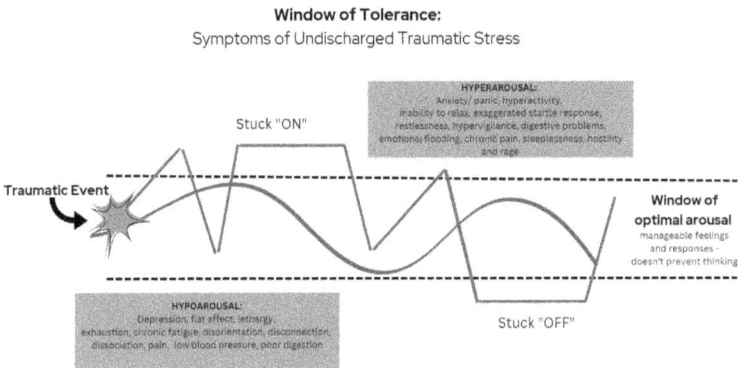

Window of Tolerance:
Symptoms of Undischarged Traumatic Stress

HYPERAROUSAL:
Anxiety/ panic, hyperactivity, inability to relax, exaggerated startle response, restlessness, hypervigilance, digestive problems, emotional flooding, chronic pain, sleeplessness, hostility and rage

Stuck "ON"

Traumatic Event

Window of optimal arousal
manageable feelings and responses - doesn't prevent thinking

HYPOAROUSAL:
Depression, flat affect, lethargy, exhaustion, chronic fatigue, disorientation, disconnection, dissociation, pain, low blood pressure, poor digestion

Stuck "OFF"

Figure 2. The Window of Tolerance.

---

[10] Graphic designed by author based on information adapted from Pat Ogden, Kekuni Minton, and Clare Pain, *Trauma and the Body: A Sensorimotor Approach to Psychotherapy* (New York: W. W. Norton & Company, 2006); Stephen W. Porges, *The Polyvagal Theory: Neurophysiological Foundations of Emotions, Attachment, Communication, and Self-Regulation* (New York: W. W. Norton & Company, 2011); Siegel, *The Developing Mind.*

An example of this might be when Jessie, the subject from our earlier vignette, both witnessed and experienced domestic violence and physical assault at the hands of his father. Jessie's brain and body learned to be hypervigilant because he never knew what his father's behavior would be like when he came home. Jessie's body was primed for survival responses regardless of when they would show up. Once the abuse occurred, Jessie would become activated into a fight or flight response, or drop down into a freeze or submit response (up or down on the graph). Over time, and through numerous traumatic events, Jessie's brain and body learned to be on high alert for potential confrontation. Subsequently, Jessie learned to remove all potential for conflict with male superiors, and he tends to "shut down" when in vulnerable situations like relationships. Though this helps him avoid the potential for harm, it also eliminates the possibility of Jessie receiving comfort.

As figure 3 illustrates, Jessie's window of tolerance has been conditioned to be smaller, so now even the smallest activating trigger sends him into a survival response. His **autonomic nervous system**, which controls involuntary physiologic activity such as heart rate, blood pressure, and respiration, is regularly primed for survival responses because he has been conditioned to expect pain, danger, and fear. Subsequent traumatic events then continue to sensitize him, making his window of tolerance smaller so that he can react quicker. In addition, his responses become more extreme in an attempt to keep him safe. This was a great adaptive response when Jessie was in constant danger. However, now that he has grown up and is in a seemingly safe environment, his nervous system still expects danger and therefore reacts as if it is right around the corner. Jessie is primed for danger and will find it even if there is none, expect that individuals have nefarious intent, and be suspicious of the longevity of stability. This is why he has a difficult time connecting with partners

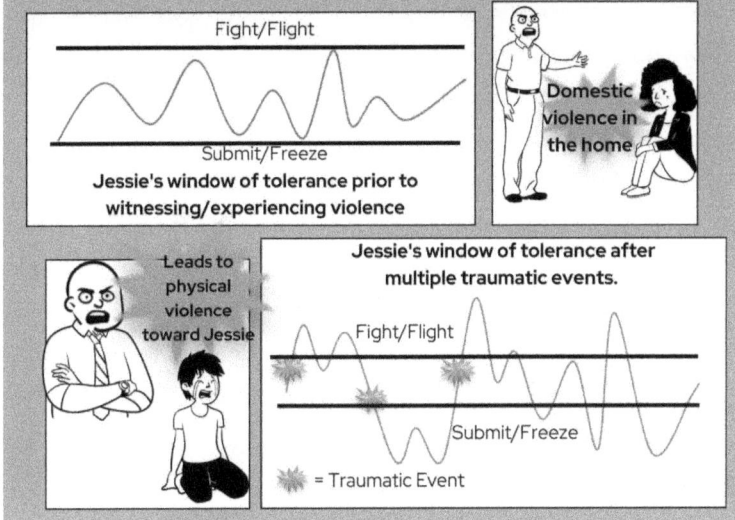

Figure 3. Jessie's Autonomic Nervous System Response
with a Lower Window of Tolerance.

and will often hold back connection or push away intimacy—he
does not trust that it is safe to love.

Resilience vs. Sensitization

Some opinions suggest that repeated exposure to an activating source will cause a type of desensitization to the activation,
meaning that being repeatedly exposed to the trigger will lessen
the response. Trauma therapists know there is more to that idea.
Repetitive activation without maintaining awareness in the present moment, and without the maintenance of safety and security,
leads to continuous flooding of the nervous system's hormones and

chemicals. In essence, it retraumatizes the individual.[11] Repeated exposure to these activating triggers, then, does not allow for desensitization; rather, it amplifies sensitization and thus body activation. As with Jessie, more exposure to activating triggers without maintaining safety and stability leads to a decreased window of tolerance, which equals further trauma responses and quicker reactivity.[12]

Essentially, what some may see as a desensitized response might actually be dissociation brought on by extreme activation. Though we may learn to diminish our presenting responses to certain triggers socially and even outwardly, internally, we may be either activated to the point of dissociation or shifting into a parts-based managerial state that does not allow us to feel the emotions attached to the activation. Either way, this is not ideal for ongoing trauma treatment and/or relational development with partners.

The Main F's

Body and brain responses to trauma or fear can take many forms. Activating forms include fight, flight, or hyper-freeze, which are primary bodily responses to a perceived threat. This body activation is experienced through the autonomic nervous system, the mobilizing and immobilizing system of your body that is broken down into two primary subcategories: the sympathetic and parasympathetic systems. The sympathetic nervous system sends those signals to the body to "Go! Fight! Run!" by increasing blood flow to muscles and

---

[11] Rajendra A. Morey et al., "Fear Learning Circuitry is Biased Toward Generalization of Fear Associations in Posttraumatic Stress Disorder," *Translational Psychiatry* 5, no. e700 (2015): 1–10, https://doi.org/10.1038/tp.2015.196.

[12] Perry, *The Boy Who Was Raised as a Dog*, 299.

lungs, dilating pupils, and increasing heart rate.[13] In a typical situation, we can feel the activation of the sympathetic nervous system when a deer runs in front of our car. After the deer runs away and we pull over to the side of the road to collect ourselves, we can feel the activation of the parasympathetic nervous system brake, the "calm down," the rest that allows our bodily functions to return to a normal rhythm. This is also prominent in the hypofreeze or feigned death responses, which include decreased blood flow to extremities and slowed heart rate. That is when the brain and body believe the threat of extreme harm or death is imminent and escape is unlikely.[14]

When an individual experiences chronic trauma, their sympathetic nervous system continuously activates. This chronic activation leads to "stuck on" or "stuck off" reactions, such as those illustrated in figure 3, minimizing their window of tolerance and making it difficult to land back into a rested state. This level of activation can also make it incredibly challenging to return to a state of connection, which requires individuals to access the **ventral vagal state**.[15] In this state, an individual can use their mobilized energy for connection and play versus fighting or fleeing.

The key difference between sympathetic activation and the ventral vagal state is safety. For example, if you try to cross the road and almost get hit by a car, you would not immediately be in the right "headspace" to make new friends or kiss your spouse, because your body would be too activated with survival energy. However, if

---

[13] Laurie Kelly McCorry, "Physiology of the Autonomic Nervous System," *American Journal of Pharmaceutical Education* 71, no. 4 (2007): 78, https://doi.org/10.5688/aj710478.

[14] Erica A. Wehrwein, Hakan S. Orer, and Susan M. Barman, "Overview of the Anatomy, Physiology, and Pharmacology of the Autonomic Nervous System," *Comprehensive Physiology* 6, no. 3 (2016):1239–1278, https://doi.org/10.1002/cphy.c150037.

[15] Porges, *The Polyvagal Theory*, 127–140.

your body is churning with energy due to excitement (like attending a football game), you are far more likely to make new friends and connect with people in a playful and meaningful way due to the lack of potential threat of harm. Translating that scenario into your everyday life, if you are chronically activated with survival energy due to complex PTSD or a significant history of trauma, you are inherently going to have much more difficulty calming your body and brain enough to form meaningful relationships, simply because you don't feel safe enough.

Individually, this can show up in many ways. For me, depending on the activation, I tend to react in a freeze state initially. If my child were running into the road, for example, I would not be able to move. Everything would be in slow motion for me, and I could not even think enough to respond. My wife, on the other hand, would respond in a fight-based way initially, running toward the road to protect our child. At a time like this, my freeze response could be misinterpreted as indifference or lack of care, when in actuality, it is a basic bodily response that I don't have much control over.

Relationally, this can play out in similar ways. As seen in the foreword, if my wife and I are arguing and I am trying to get her to hear me, I may follow her around the house trying to explain my position. Because of her trauma history and her survival responses, she may feel trapped or cornered in these situations. Her flight response kicks in, and she will walk away. My pursuit of her only intensifies this response, causing her to feel more and more pressure to get out of a situation that, because of her history, feels dangerous or scary. The part of her brain that can sort through past trauma versus current stressors is not online to help her delineate, and therefore she responds as if the past is the present. She first tries to put physical space between us, and then she uses words to push me away if needed—all as a body-based trauma response to reestablish safety.

Fawning

The fawn response is different from the other Fs in that it is both inherent and cultivated. **Fawning** is a vagal/physiological response that involves a shutdown and numbing of the dorsal vagus nerve, causing us to pull away from a fight/flight/freeze option when harm is eminent and escape is not possible. At the same time, this overstimulates the ventral vagal response of connection and hyper-attunement to other's needs. In short, fawning involves people-pleasing to the degree that an individual disconnects from their own emotions, sensations, and needs in order to meet the needs of others and maintain safety.[16]

Fawning can develop in childhood when a child is put in the position to put others' needs before their own on a consistent basis. Often these children must withhold significant expressions of feelings such as sadness, anger, or fear to avoid being harmed or neglected by a caregiver.[17] As a result, the child rationalizes the situation by telling themselves that the parent "is an adult" and "knows what's best." Therefore, the child starts to believe the negative messages and internalizes the negative beliefs about themselves as "no good," "a disappointment," and/or "worthless." This can turn into deeply rooted self-criticism and self-loathing and become the root of codependence in adulthood. Fawning can also occur when there is a less obvious but just as valid threat to security and safety, such as parental disapproval, abandonment, or dismissal.

---

[16] Pete Walker, "Codependency, Trauma and the Fawn Response," accessed February 11, 2023, http://www.pete-walker.com/codependencyFawnResponse.htm.

[17] Jakub Owca, "The Association between a Psychotherapist's Theoretical Orientation and Perception of Complex Trauma and Repressed Anger in the Fawn Response" (PhD diss., The Chicago School of Professional Psychology, 2020), 1–24, https://www.proquest.com/openview/83faad71347dae7bba4d3b130d083e88/1?pq-origsite=gscholar&cbl=18750&diss=y.

Example:

Initially, Hannah tried to seek out her mother's comfort when she was sad, felt scared, or needed reassurance. However, her mother did not provide reassurance and instead would minimize Hannah's feelings, turn away or change the subject when Hannah brought up difficult or emotionally charged topics, and would even blatantly ignore Hannah if she was crying. When Hannah got good grades, was dating a popular boy from church, or received recognition for her appearance, though, her mother would provide positive attention and validation. Hannah began to understand that in order to get her mother's approval, avoid emotional abandonment, or not have her presence dismissed, she needed to show only certain emotions and act only in specific ways. Ultimately, this diminished Hannah's true sense of self in return for comfort from her mother, who had significant difficulty of her own expressing and validating emotions. Hannah began to hate "vulnerability" or outward expressions of emotion, because she connected those to feelings of fear of abandonment and/or rejection. To parts of Hannah, emotional expression no longer "served a purpose" and "was more trouble than it was worth." When Hannah started to have romantic feelings toward a girl from school, she pushed them down and began hating those thoughts and feelings—rejecting her true self to avoid her mother's rejection.

Relationally, fawning can be seen in interpersonal adult relationships when a partner consistently "gives in" to another partner out of trauma-laced fear of retaliation or expression of emotions. When that happens, one partner sees the other as a threat to their physical or emotional safety (or the safety of the relationship). This learned response can also present as difficulty saying "no" or difficulty setting firm boundaries within a relationship, and in interpersonal domestic violence relationships, as a way for the victim to separate the trauma from their attachment to the perpetrator. In these situations, it can be too painful for the victim to see their primary attachment figure as the same individual that could hurt them significantly, so parts of them compartmentalize the pain from the attachment. In actuality, they are still minimizing their own needs for the primary goal of safety. "Fawners" can also take on a parental role toward their partner's emotional needs and can have a sense of loss of identity when in adult relationships.

Fawning and Queer Identity

Living in a world where being queer is not always accepted, and wherein we receive large-scale messages that indicate anything from lack of support to homicidal action towards the queer community, there is a perpetual and insidious implication of danger. Our brains naturally scan the environment hundreds of times a minute under normal circumstances, but with repeated trauma, they learn to scan even faster. In so doing, the brain recognizes that there are innumerable options to trigger fear-based body responses.[18] Combining the exponentially higher risk of queer identity with your body's natural need to survive cultivates a dire need to develop fawning behaviors as a survival mechanism. Childhood messages we may have received from environmental homophobia and transphobia could cause us

---

[18] Bessal A. van der Kolk, "Trauma and Memory," *Journal of Psychiatry and Clinical Neurosciences* 52, no. S1 (1998): S52–S64, https://doi.org/10.1046/j.1440-1819.1998.0520s5S97.x.

to internalize and suppress queer identity for the comfort of others and safety of ourselves. This can enhance difficulty and fear of coming out, increase internalized homophobia, and even have implications for the development and maintenance of queer relationships. Difficulty with being authentic, fighting internal and external messages of self-worth, and having decreased access to external trusted and safe support can impact an individual's ability and willingness to have healthy boundaries and advocate for their needs. It can even have levels of intimacy that are not laced with indoctrinated feelings of shame.

My Example:

The nurse at my doctor's office is chatty as she takes my blood pressure, and she asks me if I've been feeling sick, have traveled out of the country, or am sad. It isn't until she says, "I see you're married. What does your husband do?" that the energy changes. I could lie. I could say that "he" is a therapist. I could use neutral pronouns and say, "my spouse" or "they." Or I could out myself to this stranger, in this little room with harsh overhead lights, and hope she has a supportive reaction.

I go for it. "My wife is a therapist." Silence. Silence so deafening that the invasive "rrriiippp" of the blood pressure cuff is a welcome reprieve.

"Oh," is all she says before collecting her things and informing me that the doctor will be right in.

The door closes and I'm left with shame, guilt, anger, and resentment. But not toward her... toward myself. *I feel shame* for loving a woman. Society told me I should feel that way and that has been inherently baked into our current political climate.

> *I feel guilt* that I could, for one second, feel ashamed of the best and truest relationship I've ever been in. I love my wife with all of my being. *I feel angry* with myself for having the initial reaction of shame. *I feel weak* that I let a stranger make me question my life, my happiness. And *I feel resentment* that my mind already started making excuses for the nurse—reasons why her deafening silence could have been acceptable.

In this example, I'm cycling through learned responses of dulling myself down for the comfort of others, both in the presence of the nurse and individually, after the nurse leaves. Societal messages of shame and fear led to my hesitation of disclosure, which was reinforced by the nurse's reaction and further perpetuated these learned fawning behaviors and beliefs. Internally, I was torn between being authentic and being safe, or between being honest and being accepted.

It is doubtful that future patients are likely to answer screening questions accurately, or report domestic violence by a same-sex partner or a non-heterosexual sexual assault, if there is a concern related to the nurse's response. The shame, self-blame, and judgment related to these topics is profound enough, even before adding the dimension of queer identity or non-hetero trauma.

Trauma Memory

Trauma memory is not like typical memory. Memories of what you ate for dinner last night or a review of a recently seen movie are stored in a different part of the brain than memories related to trauma. Trauma-related memory is stored in the part of the brain most related to short-term memory so that it can respond appropriately when triggered by outside stimuli. This allows the body and the brain to react accordingly if something sounds, smells, or feels like something they have experienced before and is associated with trauma. Because of this, trauma memory tends to be more sensation-based as opposed to chronological.[19] For example, an individual might remember the way their attacker smelled, or the color of the car that was driving by while they were being attacked, but they might not remember the time they left for the party, what they said to the individual, or what they did after the attack. Once activated, the part of the brain that stores memory in a chronological way is minimally accessible. Therefore, the "printer" in the brain is printing out things not as the script happens, but instead as a strobe light of sensation.

Because of the lack of chronology, it is at times difficult for the brain to distinguish between past and present danger. If something sounds like, smells like, or incites an emotional response that is similar to something that has been known to be dangerous, the body responds in accordance with the perceived and remembered level of threat. Therefore, when I raise my voice, or when my wife or I raise our voices at each other, our brains pick up that cue and respond as if a past threat is standing right in front of us.

Another facet of trauma memory to consider is the phenomenon of **betrayal blindness**, first researched by Jennifer Freyd, wherein the lived experiences are not cataloged as betrayal or trauma in the moment.[20] This is the brain's internal coping mechanism to guard against things that threaten the internal system of safety. If a person were to truly see the reality of the trauma while still being involved in it, it could threaten the very relationships on which that person

---

[19] Pat Ogden and Mason A. Sommers, "Sensorimotor Psychotherapy Training for Mental Health Professionals, Level I: Trauma," Sensorimotor Psychotherapy Institute, Professional Training Program, accessed February 12, 2020, https://sensorimotorpsychotherapy.org/curriculum/trauma/.

[20] Jennifer Freyd, *Blind to Betrayal: Why We Fool Ourselves We Aren't Being Fooled* (New Jersey: Wiley, 2013).

depends. This can happen in parent–child relationships when a child is not able to see how traumatic their childhood is until their parent passes away and they are no longer dependent on that relationship. It can also occur in interpersonal relationships when there is such a deep connection, vulnerability, and interdependence that the *knowing* or *acknowledgment* of the betrayal is a direct threat to the sense of relational survival.

Forgetting or "not seeing" a situation is not a conscious choice, but a freeze-based survival mechanism. Often, it is not until we can help grow a person's internal strength, confidence, and sense of self—to the point that they are able to look fully at what is happening in their relationship and survive it emotionally—that they are able to remember or acknowledge the depth of the betrayal.

The concepts of memory gaps and sensory memory processing are important to remember for a variety of reasons and in a variety of settings. When asking an individual about their trauma history or inquiring about a traumatic event, their inability to repeat back the chronological order of events is *not* indicative of their truth and should *not* be used in a way to discredit them or their memories by any means. We often see media depictions of survivors being interviewed by various agencies and having those survivors discredited for "changing stories," "inconsistencies," or "missing pieces." Instead of this being grounds for a disputed report, this should instead provide credibility to the story because this is exactly how trauma memory is stored and processed. In a relational dynamic, it can be frustrating for a partner when an individual reports minimal memory of an event but has incredibly activating triggers.

We have to remember that it is not our job to validate the event or experience because we have complete understanding of what happened and/or screen it for correctness. Instead, it is our job to support and provide empathetic understanding and compassion.

Trauma Tree

Understanding the way a tree grows is helpful in understanding how trauma moves through our beliefs, sense of self, and presenting symptomology. First, the seed is planted, which is the traumatic event. Sometimes it is a single-event trauma, but if there is complex trauma involved, such as multiple traumas, ongoing trauma, or betrayal, fertilizer gets poured onto that seed, expediting its growth and heartiness. After the trauma occurs, the development of the impact takes hold. Roots grow deep into the soil in the form of beliefs about self-worth, beliefs about the world, blame/shame, and negative cognitions about varying topics related to the trauma (e.g., "I'm not worth loving," "I'm not worth protection," or "Love is expressed through pain"). The sprouts above the surface grow as well, and these turn into branches, the major themes of how we are impacted by the trauma in the "real world." Next, the leaves form, which are the symptoms we experience every day. Often, we go to a doctor or therapist to treat these "leaves" and are either prescribed various medical tests and medications or told that there is no medical explanation for our symptoms or very real pain. These symptoms are body-stored trauma, and that triggers responses that have nowhere to go in the moments of pain, control, or danger.

Example:

Chronic gastrointestinal issues can result from shutdowns and hyperactivity, depending on the body's reaction to danger. It makes logical sense that if you continue being activated due to hypervigilance and chronic triggers, the stop-start, stop-start of the gastrointestinal system will result in major issues.

This example can be generalized to a wide variety of other chronic illnesses during which the body gets stuck in survival mode and causes unbalanced physiology. The body's internal mechanism for maintaining homeostasis by turning off and on various physiological mechanisms as a way of responding to anticipated stressors is called **allostasis**.[21] Prolonged exposure to stress increases the body's response and anticipation systems, thereby creating an increase in allostatic load resulting from chronic nervous system dysregulation, which can then present as fibromyalgia, postural orthostatic tachycardia syndrome, chronic fatigue, depression, anxiety/panic attacks, chronic headaches and migraines, irritable bowel syndrome, and cardiovascular disease.[22] Essentially, it means overusing stress response systems to the point of burnout and multi-system impact.

All of this can result in trauma survivors being in and out of the medical system with a variety of seemingly unconnected symptomology, and at times being ostracized, judged, or rejected as being "medication seeking," "a frequent flier," or "attention seeking"—all messages of invalidation that reinforce our original cognitions, systemic betrayals, and "roots." Understanding this connection between trauma and physical/emotional/relational symptomology is essential in the treatment of trauma and the validation of body-based experiences, and that is the first step in healing.

Figure 4 depicts a Trauma Tree, with trauma at the ground level, self-talk/learned negative cognitions below the line, and self-expression or personification of those cognitions above the line.

---

[21] Bruce S. McEwon, "Stress, Adaptation, and Disease: Allostasis and Allostatic Load," *Annals of the New York Academy of Sciences* 840, no. 1 (1998): 33–44, https://doi.org/10.1111/j.1749-6632.1998.tb09546.x.

[22] Karen R. Word, Suzanne H. Austin, and John C. Wingfield, "Allostasis Revisited: A Perception, Variation, and Risk Framework," *Frontiers in Ecology and Evolution* 10 (2022): 1–10, https://doi.org/10.3389/fevo.2022.954708.

Throughout the book, we will focus on identifying all these parts so we can recognize that by changing our root stories, we can change the color and function of our leaves.

Addiction
Posture/Chiropractic
Self-Sabotaging
GI Issues
Depression
Self Critical
Issues with sex
Hypervigilance
Fawning
Rigidity
Emotional Dysregulation
Headaches
Relationship Conflict
Anxiety
Fear of commitment
Perfectionism
Fear of Abandonment
Oppositional Behaviors
Difficulty feeling/trusting love
Eating Disorders
Food Hoarding

Environmental Trauma Generational/Historical
Physical, Emotional, Sexual Abuse   Religious Trauma War
Identity Trauma   Developmental Trauma

I don't deserve safety
Love = Pain
I'm unlovable
People can't be trusted
The world isn't safe
My achievements = my worth
I'm better off alone   I'm worthless

@your.queer.therapist

Figure 4. The Trauma Tree.

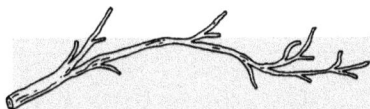

Digging Deeper: Your Trauma Tree Activity

1) What are your main traumas that you can identify? What planted those seeds of traumatic response?

_____

_____

_____

_____

2) What are your "roots" (those beliefs about yourself and the world that resulted from the trauma)?

_____

_____

_____

_____

3) What are your "leaves" (everyday physical or emotional symptoms that you notice)?

_____

_____

_____

_____

Fill in Your Own Trauma Tree

Fill in your own Trauma Tree. Identify the main trauma(s) that occurred, the negative beliefs that developed (roots), and how those show up in your everyday life (leaves).

@your.queer.therapist

Chapter 2
Identity Development and Attachment

I'm not sure which matters more—where the seed comes from, or where it takes root and grows.
– Zetta Elliott, *A Wish After Midnight*

As we develop and grow, we not only meet certain physical milestones and achieve specific growth measurements, but also establish a sense of who we are in the world. We determine what socially normative and expected behaviors are, discover what language is and what it's used for, and learn to label things like "table," "food," and "love." We take in information from many external sources and decide what we are "supposed" to do and who we are "supposed" to be. I often have clients who come into my office recognizing the "unlearning" they must do in order to be their true and authentic selves. While this reckoning occurs with cisgender (gender identity aligning with sex assigned at birth) and heterosexual individuals, I have found that so many more queer folks have been indoctrinated with the "supposed to" and "not supposed to" of love, attraction, and expression.

The development of our queer selves goes so far beyond our professional "callings" or our "brands," instead becoming a deeper dive into seeing where the messages were received and what messages were poisonous to our true authenticity. I have clients ask how in the world they are supposed to excise integral, baked-in parts of their development or upbringing without losing key pieces of themselves. The answer is simple: *you don't*. The cake is baked, my friends. Messages of "good," "bad," "should," and "have to," as well as sexist, racist, classist, ableist, colonialist, and all the "ists," have been the eggs, flour, and sugar making up the cake that is you. Doing the work to call ourselves out and challenge the internalized messaging we all have within us is not only the first step in moving forward with more awareness and humility globally, but also the way we heal from our own baked-in traumas.

"Doing the work" manifests in a variety of ways, but ultimately it is a three-step process. First, throughout chapters 1 and 2, we are starting to identify patterns, reactions, and the "why's" of our brains, bodies, and relationships. Second, within chapters 3 and 4, we will begin identifying those responses and reactions in the moment to catch ourselves reacting in certain ways, recognize that our responses may be due to our own internal "stuff," and challenge automatic thoughts at the time of the stressor or trigger. Third, in chapter 5 and beyond (as well as the workbook prompts throughout the book), we will work on building in ways to nurture ourselves so that we don't have such big, raw, incongruous reactions and internalizations in the future.

The first step begins with learning more about how we learned what was "safe" or "dangerous" and how that has played out in our everyday lives.

Neuroception

Neuroception is an individual's ability to determine safety based on internal and external stimuli.[23] When we are children, we rely on caregivers and trusted adults to provide a blueprint of what is safe and unsafe as we explore and experience the world. The scary sounds that come with storms can provide an incredibly activating and fearful response to a child who has never experienced that before. It is our caregiver's job to provide soothing reassurance that those noises are not associated with things that are dangerous: "It's okay, Sweetie. It's just thunder. You're safe and Mommy's here." When that happens, the child's brain stores those noises in the "safe and okay" category so that when they come up again, the child knows how to respond.

This applies not only to sensations and sensory input, but to normalizing emotional responses and reactions as well. If we are anxious about starting school, for example, we feel the anxiety manifest physically as butterflies in our stomach or heat in our faces. We then bring it to the attention of our caregivers who can provide reassurance and normalization that "things are going to be okay, and going to a new school provokes anxiety in everyone." When we learn that our internal processing of events and stimuli matches the reassurance of our parents and the situation, we are essentially learning a language: how to process incoming information. That language teaches us how to filter through unknown experiences to determine our level of safety. We calm our body by reassuring ourselves that either the unknown sensory input is "safe" or that the situation is "scary for everyone, but I can get through it." We might also categorize things in the "unsafe" category, like running with scissors or stranger danger.

---

[23] Mona Delahooke, *Beyond Behaviors: Using Brain Science and Compassion to Understand and Solve Children's Behavioral Challenges* (Eau Claire, WI: PESI Publishing & Media, 2019), 20–21.

Conversely, if our caregivers don't provide nurturing or consistent messages related to external and internal stimuli, we can learn *not* to trust our environment or our own internal processes of the environment. For example, in cases of child abuse, when internally the child feels incredibly anxious and rejects a parent who may have hurt them, if another parent reassures them that "it is okay," that the perpetrating parent is "fine and to be trusted," or the child is "making a big deal about nothing," that child learns to *not* trust their internal judgment. They then have a difficult time discerning safe from unsafe relationships in the future. After all, the parent is supposed to be "the expert" and trusted to tell the truth. In essence, that child's brain is thinking, "If I'm feeling anxious and distrustful of my mom because she hurt me, but my dad says it's okay, I can't trust my own anxiety because it doesn't match what my parents have told me." Relationally, this can be problematic for adults as well. If the child does not have a blueprint for what is safe or unsafe, if they don't know how to internally process their feelings of discomfort related to a situation, the parent may either become overly reliant on their partner to provide that regulation or be somewhat disorganized in their own ability to process it.

As a queer individual in a world that is primary cisgendered and heterosexual, the idea of safety and trust can be even trickier. The messages we receive from society are disorganized, to say the least. On one hand, we could be told that we are accepted: "Look at the Equality of Marriage Act!" "I don't discriminate, I have a gay cousin that I love!" And while these messages are not *true* acceptance or celebration, they are, at times, the presumed "proof" of societal acceptance. On the other hand, the statistics for assault based on sexual orientation or gender identity are incredibly disproportionate. So what are we to believe? Should we believe that walking down the street and holding our partner's hand is going to be safe, or do we hide because of the anxiety we feel inside? Anxiety says hide, but society says safe.

This is another example of how our bodies and brains are programmed to keep us safe: it is safer to *not* trust everything and stay alive than it is to trust the potentially untrustworthy and end up hurt. So, sometimes we hide and don't necessarily need to, and sometimes we hide and think that was a good choice, because that couple over there was *not* hiding and just got heckled. Other times, the body and brain tell us to stay hidden because the world is too unpredictable, and safety is better than the potential for pain.

Attachment

The central idea of attachment is that primary caregivers who are available and responsive to an infant's needs enable that child to explore the world with a sense of safety and freedom, knowing that their caregiver is dependable and will meet their needs.[24] When a parent is erratic, absent, dangerous, or inconsistent in meeting the needs of a child, the child does not develop a sense of security or trust that their needs (basic and emotional) are going to be met. These children can develop **insecure attachment**. There are several types and subtypes of insecure attachment styles, but the three most basic styles are avoidant, anxious, and disorganized.

Avoidant Attachment

With **avoidant attachment**, the caregiver was absent, neglectful, or harmful to the point that the child learned they could not rely on the caregiver to get their needs met; the caregiver may have even

---

[24] Mary D. Salter Ainsworth, "Attachments and Other Affectional Bonds Across the Life Cycle," in *Attachment Across the Life Cycle*, eds. Colin M. Parkes, Joan Stevenson-Hinde, and Peter Marris (London: Routledge, 1993), 33–51.

punished the child for relying on them. The child learns that relying on others to meet their emotional needs is unsafe and may push away their caregivers and future partners. This often appears in relationships as someone who is afraid of getting "too close," is "emotionally closed off" or "rigid," or leaves or shuts down during arguments or when relationships get too deep or serious. Think back to Jessie from chapter 1. Jessie's father was abusive to his mother and eventually abusive toward him. When Jessie grew up, he had an aversion to connection. His partners describe him as "aloof" or "closed off," and he gets close to a partner only to pull away or sabotage the intimacy when he feels too vulnerable. Like other individuals with avoidant attachment, Jessie is hesitant to reach out and connect to others because historically, his relational blueprint taught him that relying on others was not safe, and he usually ended up managing his own needs.

Anxious Attachment

Anxious attachment develops when a child's caregiver was unpredictable in meeting the child's needs. This caregiver might have been kind one moment and rejective the next. Subsequently, the child grew up never knowing when the "kind caregiver" was going to show up and clung to them when they did. An adult with this attachment style can have great distress around relationships, being anxious that the relationship will end or that the partner might leave. These individuals usually have lower self-esteem and think very highly of their partner regardless of whether they are a healthy match, which can lead to anxiously attached individuals staying in harmful relationships much longer than individuals with other attachment styles. As children, these adults also learned that caregivers who are unpredictable are also more likely to respond to and meet the need of a child in distress. In adulthood, this may manifest as adult partners who receive diagnoses of borderline personality disorder or another affective, seemingly "dramatic" behavior when they fear abandonment or rejection.

Example:

Darren's father left when he was young, and his mother worked doubles to pay the bills. She was not around much, and when she was, she was often too tired to engage and slept all the time. Sometimes, Darren would wake up in the morning to the smell of pancakes and bacon. He would run downstairs to find his mother smiling and being engaged. They would eat together and she would play trucks with him. She might even tuck him in at night and read him a story. Then, for several days, she would work and be too exhausted to even take him to school. The only time Darren knew he could depend on his mother was when he was sick. She would stay home from work, make him soup, snuggle with him, and gently brush his hair back from his forehead while singing him a lullaby. Sometimes Darren would pretend to be sick so that he could spend time with his mother. Over time, he developed genuine stomachaches and fainting spells that no doctor could explain.

As an adult, Darren now has terrible "separation anxiety" from his partner. He will often call or text several times in a row if his partner does not answer. Sometimes he will assume things about his partner, such as believing he is cheating or that he got into a car accident. When Darren gets really scared, his stomachaches come back. Often, the only way he feels safe is when his partner is there, and he texts his partner whenever he does not feel good or feels like he is going to faint. In those moments, Darren's need to connect is so intense that he becomes desperate to feel it and genuinely thinks he might explode if he cannot reach his partner.

These events can be interpreted as attempts to avoid abandonment, which they are. But it is not an adult Darren who is manipulating the situation to control or hurt, it is the younger version of Darren that remembers the feeling of not knowing when he would get his needs met by his mother. And that feeling echoes in his current relationship with his partner.

Disorganized Attachment

Disorganized attachment involves a caregiving scenario in which there is both comfort and terror for the child. In this environment, the child does not know how to respond and alternates between disconnection and fear. In relationships, this can show up as heightened responses to tension, abandonment, closeness, and rejection. Adults with disorganized attachment desire relationships, but because their relationships were unsafe and could not be trusted in the past, they have difficulty trusting them in the present.

Example:

Jake's father left when Jake was three, and Jake's mother had a variety of boyfriends before she married Scott. At first, things seemed okay. His mom was happier, she did not have to work as much, and Scott seemed nice enough. Jake's mom had always taken care of Jake, making sure he had enough to eat and that they never got evicted. She was kind and warm.

When Scott and Jake's mom first got drunk together, they were funny—dancing around and laughing. But as time went on, the funny turned mean and the laughs turned to screams. Scott would hit Jake's mom, throw things, and make threats. Sometimes, Jake's mom would hide or come into Jake's room and make sure he was okay. Other times, she would get mad and throw things too. Eventually, she started hitting Jake, who never knew what to expect in his household. The person who was capable of nurturing and making him feel safe was also the person who was terrified of her husband and could be terrifying toward Jake.

As an adult, Jake now varies between extremes of wanting connection with his partner and pushing his partner away. He gets suspicious of his partner's true feelings, can sabotage the relationship, and then quickly try to mend it by any means necessary.

Often, partners of individuals with disorganized attachment don't know what to expect because they don't know how their partner(s) will respond. The disorganization that the traumatized individual feels is so ingrained and their safety of attachment so disjointed that their responses are just as unpredictable.

Digging Deeper: Attachment Activity

Understanding your primary attachment style is a key ingredient in understanding your thoughts, behaviors, and relationships. From the examples above, do you have a "style" that resonates with you more than the others? Think back to your previous relationships. Was there a way you typically responded when you felt vulnerable? Did you pull away? Did you rush toward your partner? Did the foundation of your relationship feel really shaky anytime there was conflict? Recognizing that these responses were a direct result of your attachment style and your internalized fear of connection can help build understanding of your behaviors and the behaviors of your partner. Where did that fear come from? Was there a person in your history that you could not rely on for nurturing, safety, or connection? That person is usually not your current partner, and the missteps of the past are likely bleeding over into your current life. What are some ways your current partner _does_ support you? Nurture you? Show up? When you are feeling vulnerable, do you end up pushing your partner away instead of getting your needs of connection met? Even though it feels scary, how might your partner respond if you leaned into the vulnerability and told them you were having a difficult time?

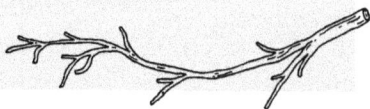

Attachment Trauma

It should be noted that while most of the discussion in this book relates attachment and attachment trauma to a parent–child relationship, attachment can also develop between partners, friends, other caregivers, and anyone with whom there is an exchange of connection, vulnerability, or trust of getting needs met. Therefore, attachment trauma can manifest in all those varying types of relationships as well. This can range from acts of significant physical or sexual abuse, to an emotionally absent parent, to a caregiver who puts someone in a role of being an emotional support or equal or perpetrates domestic violence, rejection, or betrayal.

In situations like these, children cannot rely on their parents for emotional nurturing and support when they are still learning about the world and developing as individuals. This lack of predictability, whether it be due to power dynamics, substance abuse, or something more physical, can impact a child's ability to trust that their needs are going to be met. Therefore, the parent teaches the child how important (or unimportant) their needs are, how much they should rely on others, and what they need to do to get their needs met in the future, which impacts the trajectory of their life right from the get-go.

Example:

You are an eight year old who comes home from school after an incredibly embarrassing event happened. You go to your parents for support, and your parent had such a difficult day that they are not emotionally available and start telling you about their recent heartbreak. Pushing down your need for support and safety, you grab a tissue for your parent, hold them while they cry, and don't bring up your hard day. You absorb the feelings of rejection you feel by them not being available and learn that your feelings are not a priority.

While this may be a one-time situation, if it continues to become the norm and you don't feel like your needs can get met on a regular basis or are responsible for caring for the emotional needs of your parent, your attachment to that parent is impacted. It also impacts your ability to get your needs met, have faith in their ability to protect and support you, and believe what they teach you about what you can and cannot work through. This attachment then permeates the rest of your relationships going forward. With instances of significant trauma during which there are one or more major betrayals in the form of physical or sexual abuse, this lack of trust and betrayal is not necessarily insidiously built over time, but radically wounded through that event. The attachment impact can be the same and reflect similar patterns in adulthood. The complexity of developmental betrayal trauma is such that it can also impact sense of self, self-esteem, worth, guilt and shame, and negative cognitions.

Negative Cognitions

As you just learned, experiences and messages of worth from caregivers become our inner voices and narrate the stories we tell ourselves about the world. These cognitions then fuel our subsequent thoughts about ourselves and our behaviors. Sometimes negative cognitions can be compounded by societal pressures and/or exacerbate preexisting issues that can quickly spiral into a litany of negative thoughts, behaviors, and beliefs. In short, negative cognitions are the direct result of trauma, including why it happened, whose fault it was, and the likelihood of it happening again. These spirals are fueled by those messages and blueprints we have received from others. This can happen during childhood, throughout adult relationships and friendships, or simply via a message received from a person whose opinion you care about to some extent (e.g., a parent, a boyfriend or girlfriend, your best friend, the "cool kids" at school). Your brain then stores these messages in a "folder" as "evidence" for society at large, further building a case for the negative thoughts about yourself through which you filter incoming information.

Example:

When Samantha was very young, her mother told her that she needed to be "pretty" to be "popular" after Samantha's father cheated on her mother with a younger woman. This message of "beauty equals worth" impacted Samantha in such a way that when she was 10 and was not invited to her friend's birthday party, she assumed it was because her hair was red, since everyone else had blonde hair. In addition, Samantha was not as "skinny" as the other girls, so when her friend Rachel asked her what size shirt she wore, Samantha assumed that Rachel was being critical of her weight. Samantha isolated herself from Rachel and her other friends to avoid the teasing that she was sure would happen. Eventually, her friends stopped inviting her to do things. While Samantha assumed this was because they had not deemed her "worthy," it was in fact because she had pulled away from them. The story she told herself (that they were rejecting her) motivated her withdrawal, thus actually *causing* her friends to pull away.

Throughout Samantha's development, increasingly more gets added to her "beauty equals worth" folder. When a girlfriend breaks up with her, when she gets fired, when she gets a double-take glance from a stranger on the subway, Samantha looks at each interaction through the lens of assuming it is negatively reflective of her appearance. Eventually, Samantha develops disordered eating, alternating between long periods of restriction and bingeing. Each interaction with another individual during which Samantha feels slighted is matched with periods of self-loathing and restriction. Each positive comment she gets for her appearance then reinforces her cognitions and her disordered eating.

Ultimately, Samantha is stuck in a trauma-response spiral: "Those girls who were whispering were talking about me and laughing at my outfit. They probably think I'm too fat to wear this. They're right. I shouldn't be wearing this. Who do I think I am? I'm disgusting. I'm going on a diet tomorrow. I should probably not eat dinner tonight or breakfast tomorrow. I should take my name off the list of interviews for the promotion since they probably don't want a slob for an executive."

As we can see in figure 5, the initial trauma of her father's betrayal caused Samantha's mother to project her hurt onto Samantha by way of messages that beauty equals worth, which equates to not getting left, hurt, rejected, or abandoned if you look a certain way. That message became Samantha's internal sounding board, which was compounded by her fear of being left, the way her father left her mother. She began believing that if she could only be "good enough" for someone to stay, that would ensure she would never get abandoned and would never be hurt. In addition, if she recognized that there was a possibility of being rejected and she had minimal control over it, she would intentionally avoid the situation completely (withdrawing her name from the possible promotion for fear and/or assumption of rejection).

Figure 5. Samantha's Trauma-Response Spiral.

Those negative cognitions (beliefs) we develop about ourselves and our stories can significantly impact the way we look at the world, not only individually, but also in all the interactions we have with our partners. If Samantha puts on fun makeup and wears a new outfit and her partner fails to tell her that she looks lovely, Samantha may wrongly assume that her partner no longer finds her attractive. Because of her blueprints of negative beliefs related to her "evidence" folder, Samantha may start a fight or pull away. Figure 5 illustrates how Samantha's beliefs impact her behavior and how that behavior actually causes Alex to pull away—something Samantha is trying to avoid.

Chapter 2—Check In

Before you start this exercise, as well as throughout and after the exercise, do a check-in with yourself. Does this bring up difficult memories for you? Are there big hurts that you can feel viscerally? Where do you feel them? Are those fight/flight/freeze responses happening in your body? Are you starting to feel agitated at memories of unhappy or disturbing events or noticing parts of yourself that want to shut down or pull away? Take a moment to check in with all the parts of yourself. Remind yourself that you can put this book down at any time and that you will take a break if needed. Reassure yourself that you will listen to your body if you feel activated, and you will take a break, take a walk, connect with others, and take time to hold those little parts of you that feel like the trauma happened just yesterday. At any point in time, you can inquire within, and determine if you need to step away and take some time to center yourself, knowing you can always return.

_____

_____

_____

_____

_____

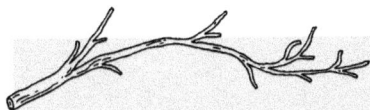

Digging Deeper: The Stories I Tell Myself

In situations like the above graphic, it is helpful to ask yourself, "What is the story I'm telling myself?" and then to do some fact checking. In this exercise, you will identify some "stories" that first pop into your head following the prompts given. Be honest. What is the first thought you have about yourself?

After you finish, try to trace those messages back to any seminal events that might have sparked the formation of your "evidence folders."

- You come home from a busy day and your spouse does not even look at you.
  Story: _____

- You are passed over for a promotion.
  Story: _____

- Your child says they would rather just hang out with friends than spend the day with you.
  Story: _____

- You call your friend, who you know is home, and they send you to voicemail.
  Story: _____

- You are chatting online with a cute person and then, all of a sudden, they "ghost" you.
  Story: _____

- Your parent comes to visit and starts asking about your "life plan."
  Story: _____

- A person passes you on the street and gives you a mean look.
  Story: _____

- A group of work colleagues who are laughing and whispering stop abruptly when you walk by.
  Story: _____

Do any of these stories hold an especially difficult belief about yourself? When did that belief start? Was there an event that sparked it?

Take a moment to think about how that event has shaped the blueprint of your beliefs. With fresh eyes, challenge those stories above with an alternative that has *nothing* to do with you.

Example: Your spouse does not look at you.

Story: They don't find me attractive anymore. I'm nothing to them but a roommate. It's only a matter of time before they get sick of me and want to end things. I'm going to pull away to try to make it hurt less when they leave.

Alternative: My spouse might've had a really long day. I should give them a few minutes and then inquire as to what's going on and how I might support them.

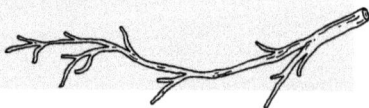

Chapter 3
Parts

We are the true roots of resistance, they declared,
and the scraggly leaves, golden flowers,
and windborne seeds.
— Rivera Sun, *The Roots of Resistance*

Everyone feels like a failure in relationships at some point, so you likely have too. Maybe it is failing to be the best parent you could be or failing to be a supportive and present partner. Perhaps it is failing to be a good communicator who fights fair and sets boundaries or failing to be someone who can apologize when warranted. When you do fail to meet and fill these roles, it can feel disheartening, exhausting, and frustrating. After all, it is not like you *want* to yell at your kids when you are stressed or zone out when your partner tries to connect with you. Understanding why we react the way we do, why we "fail," and what we can do about it is the purpose of this chapter.

What Are "Parts"?

The first step in understanding and deconstructing some of these perceived failures is recognizing that we have a multiplicity within us. Our minds and psyches are made up of various **parts**, sometimes referred to as subpersonalities, each of which have their own unique jobs based on their individual needs, wants, and beliefs.[25] Though it may sound like a confusing or even frightening concept at first, we refer to this multiplicity every day when we say things like, "A part of me wants to go to the party and be social, and another part of me wants to stay home," or "A part of me is lonely and wants to make new friends, and another part of me is anxious and fearful of rejection." These parts consciously and subconsciously exist in ways that either help or harm us as we move through life encountering experiences, challenges, and triggers. Some of our parts can help us be silly and playful, strong advocates, or caring teachers, and other parts can help protect us from hurtful things.

Each part of us functions to help navigate us through life by assisting us in filling the various roles we need to fill. Imagine getting a call from work while in the middle of your six-year-old's birthday party. There is an inherent internal shift from one energy to another because you don't want the silly and playful dad part of you to answer questions about your company's merger. This very natural and flowing state shift is an example of that "part" embodiment, which shifts depending on need. Imagine a bus full of occupants that embody different parts of you. Some parts are better at navigating city driving, and some enjoy the long expanses of rolling rural areas. Sometimes all is well on the bus while the adult part of you drives to where you need to go to navigate the day. However,

---

[25] Richard Schwartz, *No Bad Parts* (Boulder, CO: Sounds True, 2021), 12–14.

sometimes a different part of you needs to take over to assist in hairy situations.

By developing an awareness of these parts within us and how they impact the roles we embody, we can learn to give each part a voice; respond to our individual part's wants, needs, and fears; and develop an understanding of why they respond in the ways they do. This allows us to build the capacity for self-acceptance, self-compassion, and harmony within. We learn to ask ourselves, "Which part of me is driving the bus right now?"

How Our Parts Develop When Trauma Is Present

When a trauma occurs, just like any other experience that feels overwhelming, our psyches unconsciously catalog through a list of available parts to respond to the stressor. This can look like our managerial part that takes over driving the bus when a parent dies. That part helps us make all the phone calls and arrangements and work out all the details to take care of the funeral.

When we experience an interpersonal trauma or when there is not a consistent teaching about appropriate emotional reactivity, our parts begin to embody roles for maintaining safety and protection in response to perceived danger. This can also happen when trauma is repeated or significantly impactful, and the negative energy of those experiences become trapped in the body and brain, holding deep hurts of rejection, attachment wounds, heavy emotions, and developing core beliefs about worth and safety.

Example:

Pat's father told them that they were not good enough. Pat's experience of that rejection, their pain from a lack of unconditional love and emotional safety, got scorched into their memory. This pain is different from breaking an arm or stubbing a toe, because it involves a relational component and thus developed into a deeply hidden, emotionally raw nerve. As Pat moves through life, they remember those hurts and store them in their body and brain, the embodiment of those emotional burdens.

In this example, Pat's raw nerves are guarded by layers of **protector parts**. Protector parts are preexisting parts of us that step in to match the energy of a threat and, in so doing, morph into a very strong, active protector—a Hulk-level bouncer, so to speak—that is ready to keep out harm or respond should harm sneak in the back door. Our protector parts ensure that we never have to feel the hurt parts of us, that raw nerve and the beliefs that go with it, ever again. However, though they are wonderful at helping us survive *current* trauma, our parts can shift and subsequently develop into entrenched protective states that not only get us through the trauma but also continue to be very active and present even *after* the traumatic experience is over. This is when we see big reactions to seemingly small stressors as we navigate through life.

Example:

Pat goes on to work at a law firm. One day, in front of everyone, they get called out in a staff meeting by an executive. Their "raw nerve" of rejection and embarrassment gets hit. As a result, a fierce protector part takes over driving Pat's mental bus and screams at the executive, pushing away the potential for pain through active aggression and posturing and protecting Pat from further embarrassment by the executive.

As we discussed in chapter 1, trauma memory has no timeline. So, our protector parts are trying to keep us from feeling pain they are sure is just around the corner in the present day. Seemingly small triggers can have big impacts when there are learned and deeply entrenched messages of danger. Sometimes these part responses make logical sense to the outside world and sometimes they don't, but they always make sense to the parts.

Example:

Pat's reaction surprised all the other coworkers and seemed incongruent with the executive's callout. Because Pat's trauma memory has no timeline, the threat to their safety felt very present-day as opposed to a hurt from the past, so the fierce protector part took over Pat's driver's seat. Pat may lose their job, get demoted, or be reprimanded, and they may even lose the respect of their colleagues. But in the moment, Pat was unable to rationalize their responsiveness and outburst. They were too enmeshed with their part, and that part took over to respond to the threat without awareness of present-day consequences or social niceties.

Protectors—Mitigators and Reactors

Protector parts can appear in both *preventative* ways and *reactive* ways. A **preventative protector part**, which is like a manager or mitigator, might sound like, "I don't want you to feel the really terrible thing that *might* happen, so I'm going to try to control all the possible outcomes, mitigate any areas of concern, and eliminate any possibility for pain." In relationships, this might look like trying to manage the situation, control the narrative, or even mitigate a partner's activation to avoid the potential for disagreement, perceived abandonment, or feelings of guilt and shame, depending on the trigger.

A **reactive protector part** comes into play when either the mitigator (preventative part) could not fully contain the issue or the person was caught by surprise. This part might sound like, "I proactively tried to handle all my stress at work by working extra hours, making lists, and controlling my schedule, but I lost the big account anyway. I feel deep shame and sadness. To avoid feeling these raw-nerve emotions, I'm going to go to the bar and drink them away." Reactionary protector parts can take the form of depression, sleep, substance abuse, eating disorders, increased sexual encounters, avoidant or addictive behaviors—basically anything that keeps us from feeling the deeply painful emotion.

These part shifts typically parallel activated survival responses of fight, flight, freeze, fawn, or shut down states. When the body is triggered by an intense emotion, when that raw nerve is hit, the nervous system activates, which presents as a pounding heart, rapid breathing, and/or a tight chest. Because these survival responses are kicking in, part responses follow in kind: a fight part lashes out, a flight part walks out the door, a freeze or fawn part gives in regardless of the situation, and the shutdown part might trigger levels of depression or dissociation.

Figure 6 illustrates the different potential part reactions to the scenario of losing a parent.

Example:

Sam's mother is in the hospital. His proactive part steps in and tries to manage the situation by demanding quality care, calling all the doctors, and taking care of all the medical business.

SAM'S PARTS REACT TO MOM'S DEATH

Sam gets the phone call that his mom is in the hospital. His younger scared parts have big reactions of fear, loss, and abandonment.

In response, Sam's protectors emerge.

His manager part makes phone calls and speaks to the doctors – trying to control the situation.

Despite the efforts of his manager part, Sam's mother passes.

Sam's reactive part tries to avoid the pain by going to the bar and ignoring the younger parts.

Instead of allowing his protectors to ignore or push away the younger hurting parts, Sam works on turning inward and nurturing them.

Figure 6. Sam's Parts React to His Mother's Death.

This "manager" is trying to do everything in its power to push away the terrified younger parts of Sam and turn toward the outward threat: his mother's death. However, despite all the work that he did, Sam could not keep his mother from passing.

We then see Sam at the bar, where his reactive protector part takes over, avoiding the pain of the loss and further pushing away that sad and terrified younger part by means of avoidance, in this case with substance use.

In the final scene, we see Sam's adult self holding and comforting the young parts of himself that have been hurting and scared. Instead of pushing away the internal pain, Sam turns inward, toward these hurt parts of himself. This understanding and comforting of his younger hurt parts then allows Sam's "bouncers" to step back from their roles as protectors.

Since Sam's younger parts know that they can rely on Sam's adult self to comfort and care for them, they know the possibility of getting triggered is not as scary, and adult Sam takes over driving the bus.

How to Shift the Narratives

A primary goal of working with our parts is to identify our protectors and what they are protecting. Why are they there? What are they trying to prevent? What are the triggers that kick them into gear? When we can identify these things, we can work on allowing them to step out of the way of the truly transcendent adult part of us that at times get hidden by the "bouncers." This adult part (referred to as either Self, adult self, or higher self) has developed over time and inherently holds the key to calm, compassionate, curious exploration of external and internal events. While we were developing, this curious or compassionate piece of us got overshadowed by the need to be protected from harm, and our protector parts stepped in to shield those raw nerves. As fully grown humans, we can develop a better ability to protect ourselves in the present and manage our triggers as they arise.

Befriending our protectors by recognizing what they are trying to do is a great first step. This allows them to see that they can trust the adult part to keep all those big past hurts safe, protected, and more than that, unburdened from their stuck cycle of trauma responses. By allowing our protectors and past wounds to be cared for by our adult parts, we enhance the internal resources we already have. Ultimately, we develop an attachment between our adult self and our young, hurt parts. They need to trust that whatever harm, stress, or relational issues come their way, our adult self will be able to protect them, nurture them, and not abandon them. This is done not through those bouncers (protectors) pushing big feelings away, but through conscious effort of increased awareness and compassion. Effectively, we pull those young parts onto our laps and let them know we're not going anywhere, because for so long they have been locked in the shadows, pushed back, and ignored. As adults, we get to invite those protectors who have guarded the door to take a little break, grab a cup of coffee, and let us try to mend the relationships within. Imagine if we did not have to work so hard to hold back the pressure of those hurts; we could use that strength for so many other things that could bring us joy and fulfillment (see figure 7)!

Figure 7. Sam Getting Coffee with His Parts.

Take a moment to think of a situation when you felt conflicted. This could be anything, from taking a new job to attending a party with a friend. For example, a part of you may want to go to the party, but another part of you wants to stay home. Now, think of the emotion behind those parts. What is motivating the ambivalence? The part that wants to go may be afraid that your friends will be mad if you don't go. That same part may fear rejection or feel like it will "get in trouble" and therefore wants to avoid conflict. The part of you that wants to stay may fear a different kind of rejection, the kind that comes with saying the wrong thing, not reacting the way a "normal" person would, or feeling like an impostor in a crowd of "normal" people. That protector part wants you to avoid embarrassment by getting you to stay home. Each protector is trying to do just that—protect. Often, when we dig below the surface of "Eh, I don't know if I want to go or not," we can see it is actually the multiple parts inside of us that have conflicting motivations.

Thinking back to the graphics about relational dynamics and parts, we can see that parts are involved in many ways. Some parts are informed by the curious, compassionate, and calm adult self, which is the transcendent energy within, and some parts are trauma-led parts that respond and react to what they have learned are scary relational dynamics.

Parts In Relationships

In relationships, our parts can get into dances with our partner's parts. We will explore common partner part-dances in a later chapter, but for now, it is important to recognize that because our partners are the closest to us, they are the most likely to find those "vulnerable and sensitive nerves" and inadvertently trigger us.

In chapter 1, we saw examples of how parts embody roles for the sake of keeping a person safe from a perceived threat. In Susan's case, her proactive protector part cooked Mia's favorite dinner as a way to ensure Mia was in a good mood. When Mia did not respond as Susan anticipated, Susan felt rejected (big hurt) and her reactive protector took over, yelling at Mia and pushing her away. In the end, Mia asked Susan why she was reacting that way, but Susan's response was "I don't know," a common response once the initial reaction deescalates and more insight is shone upon the situation.

Digging deeper into why Susan might have reacted this way, we can see that Susan had a protector part that wanted to manage the situation by eliminating any barriers to getting its needs met. This manager part wanted to ensure that Mia was in a good mood and would be able to feel safe and connected, but even though it tried to predict Mia's behaviors and desires (by making her favorite meal), Mia was still in a bad mood and did not respond the way Susan's manager part was hoping. Because her manager part could not control the situation anymore, her reactive protector took over, responding by pushing Mia away and yelling at her, effectively rejecting Mia the way that Susan herself felt rejected. Instead of stepping back and trying to understand the situation with the transcendent adult-based insight, Susan's traumatic responses took over, stealing the microphone or driver's seat.

In my current relationship, trauma-based parts show up frequently. Thinking back to the foreword where my wife described a fight that we used to have frequently, you can see the parts in action. I had a part that felt like it *needed* to be heard and that she did not care about me or our relationship unless she stopped and paid attention. And the more it felt like it was ignored, the louder and more insistent it became, resulting in her leaving the house. She had a part that needed to get away from my words and presence, a part that did not care what it needed to say or do in order to stop me from talking. Her protector parts stepped in, and she yelled, said hateful things, and left completely. You can see her inner monologue with her parts, warring between justifying her behavior, berating her, and trying to find that adult self that could come back online to be able to have a conversation instead of an argument. Eventually, we were able to speak *for* our parts: "A part of me felt this way," instead of *from* our parts, "I hate you, get away!" This enabled a much more compassionate and calm discussion that resulted in repairing our connection.

How to Do the Work

As you are learning, though each one of us has an adult self inside, that self may not always be the one who is responding to situations or triggers in our daily lives. So, it is important to develop an understanding of the difference between our adult self and the many parts within. Identifying what is a "part" and what is not may seem like a daunting task, and it can be! Thankfully, the founders of the Internal Family Systems model identified a set of qualities to alert us to the presence of our adult selves.[26] These qualities are referred to as the eight Cs, which include compassion, creativity, curiosity, confidence, courage, calm, connectedness, and clarity. We can use these qualities to guide us by asking, "What am I leading with right now?" If the answer is one of the Cs, it is safe to assume that we are being led by our adult self. If the answer is anything else, such as judgment, indignant opinions, emotions rooted in anger, fear, or despair, then it is safe to assume a part of us is showing up and speaking out—embodied in part form—ready to protect those scared younger parts from feeling too much pain. Below is a graphic that represents the eight Cs and their potential corresponding part-led qualities.

---

[26] Richard C. Schwartz and Martha Sweezy, *Internal Family Systems Therapy* (New York: The Guilford Press, 2020), 33–48.

Self-Embodied Qualities	Part-Led Qualities
Compassion	Judgment/Coldness
Creativity	Rigidity
Curiosity	Overly Opinionated
Confidence	Fear/Shame
Courage	Defeat/Apathy
Calm	Agitation
Connectedness	Isolation
Clarity	Ambiguity

An essential distinction to make here is that trauma-led parts and protector-part responses can show up at any age, because these parts come into our lives at all different developmental stages. For those of us who experienced trauma, our brains and bodies cataloged through our lists of potential coping mechanisms. If a part did not exist that could help us, one was created or activated. Because of

Learning to identify when a part is showing up is a process. In the beginning, you may be able to recognize this only after the fact, realizing once the anger has passed that an angry part of you was speaking when you said those hurtful things to your partner. With practice, you will be able to notice these parts showing up in the moment, and eventually your adult self will be able to intervene and give these parts what they need before there is an outward blowup.

this, we may experience a feeling of being very small or childlike, and our responses may outwardly be like that of a child or teenager. We may argue with our partners using words and phrases that reflect a playground tiff, or we may refuse to participate in a family dinner like an angry teenager. We react to whatever present-day trigger was initially created at a time that embodied our younger selves. When that happens, it is a pretty solid clue that a part is driving the bus rather than our true selves.

It can be helpful to think of your parts as inner children. Some are vulnerable, terrified toddlers in need of safety and consolation, some are awkward middle schoolers who just want to belong, and others are angsty teenagers who are angry over not being heard. All of these parts need the same thing: to be reparented by your adult Self; to be seen, heard, and validated; to feel like they, and their needs, matter. Because your parts develop due to not getting your attachment needs met, they need to develop a secure attachment to you.

Thinking back to Susan, if we were able to pull her aside and dig deeper into her reactions, we might see that those protectors were actually trying to get their needs met but had limited resources in their toolboxes. If we could have a conversation with those parts, they might say something like this:

Younger/Vulnerable Part: "Needing someone is scary, but I feel lonely and unsteady. I feel like no one wants me or that if I'm too much, someone will reject me."

Proactive Manager: "If I make sure Mia is in a good mood and I set the stage for a good night, then I can step back and allow the vulnerability for connection and intimacy. But I need to make sure that everything is perfect, Mia is happy, the laundry is done, the house is cleaned, and… and… and…"
Mia does not respond as desired.

Reactive Protector: "I shouldn't have trusted that all that planning would do anything. I can't trust Mia to meet my needs. I should just push her away. I'm so ~~hurt~~ mad! I'm so ~~lonely~~ frustrated!" *Susan lashes out and pushes Mia away with her words.*

Underlying Emotion/Need Behind the Behavior: "I really want connection. I feel lonely and a little uneasy. Mia has the ability to make me feel so grounded and safe. I really want to be able to be vulnerable around her and trust that she will help me comfort myself."

So, what might we say to those parts to make them feel heard, appreciate their efforts, and allow them to know that we (the calm and compassionate eight Cs embodied in an adult) can assist in meeting the needs of that younger part? In Susan's case, her adult self can say to her younger parts, "I hear that you are scared of rejection. Rejection hurts! It's a raw nerve. And in response, you pushed Mia away. I know that I'm safe and held in this relationship, and I can be vulnerable. If my partner hurts my feelings, I know that I'll still be okay."

In these situations, our adult self has an internal conversation with our younger scared parts, reassuring them like a parent should or, unfortunately at times, like a parent did not. We have to remember that our parts will respond in parallel with our attachment style and react in an effort to avoid some of the most hurtful feelings of all: abandonment and rejection. So, because Susan has an avoidant attachment style, reaching out and trusting was already difficult for her. Feeling rejected by Mia triggered young parts of her that felt "not good enough," so she felt rejection and shame. Susan responded in sync with her attachment style and rejected Mia. However, in so doing, she pushed Mia away when what she really wanted was reassurance and connection.

What to Do with This Knowledge

Okay, so you have begun to identify your parts and notice when they are showing up in your daily life. Now what? The first step to move you out of a part-based response and back into an adult self-led response is inviting curiosity to the situation. When you notice that you are leading with a part response and then get curious about what you are experiencing, it allows you to zoom out a bit and observe your experience rather than be consumed by it.

One of the best ways that I have found to do this in my personal life is to start with compassion and curiosity. If I can be curious about why I am responding in a certain way, my awareness has already moved beyond just reacting. Sometimes my curiosity of "Why am I responding this way?" is met with a not-so-compassionate response of "Because so-and-so is acting like an ass!" Hmm… not so compassionate indeed! So, I try to turn that compassion inward instead:

Begin the same: "Why am I responding this way?"
Listen internally: "Because I'm mad!"
Process: "Why am I mad?"
"Because they pissed me off!"
"Why?"
"Because they didn't listen to me when I asked for space."
Insert compassion: "It feels really shitty when people don't respect your boundaries, doesn't it?"
Realization: "Yes, it does! I feel angry and hurt, and it reminds me of the time my mom didn't respect my boundaries and my identity. It hurt so much, and I felt so small."

In this example, using compassion and curiosity allowed me to dissect my response and identify my underlying need: to be seen and respected. This need is often something that is deeply hidden under our initial reactivity.

While this might seem easy, it is actually really hard, even after considerable awareness and practice. Sometimes it can be helpful to have some tools, cues, or reminders to assist in parsing out our parts and self-awareness and prompt us to slow down and get curious.

Tangible Tools: Cue Words

If you know you have a part of yourself that is prone to making assumptions, such as presuming that your partner is upset with you or does not care about you, you and your partner can create a cue word like "inquiry" to prompt you to take a step back.

Example 1:

After Elliot invites Rachel out for a short walk, he gets distracted and loses track of time. Rachel texts Elliot asking where they are, and Elliot's immediate part-based response is to get defensive. Elliot's protective part responds with a defensive text, having already assumed that Rachel is angry and trying to control their time.

Elliot: Geez! I'm soooorrry! Can't I have any time for myself?!

Rachel's internal dialogue: *What? Why are they responding this way? I only asked where they are because it's been well over an hour, and I wanted to make sure they were safe. I don't deserve to be talked to like this! Oh, wait. Elliot is telling themselves a story and making an assumption. I'm not going to respond from my defensive part. I'm going to use our cue word instead.*

Rachel recognizes what is happening and responds only with the word "inquiry." Based upon previous conversations and the agreement to use this cue word, Elliot knows this means Rachel is not angry or trying to control their time.

Elliot's internal dialogue: *She said "inquiry." I need to take a minute. What am I feeling right now? My jaw is tight, my fists are clenched, and my heart is racing. I feel defensive, like I need to protect or defend myself. Why am I feeling so defensive? Because she's controlling and questioning me. I didn't even do anything wrong! She has no right to be mad! Oh, wait. She said "inquiry," which means she isn't mad. This doesn't have to become a huge fight. It might feel really good to give her a piece of my mind though. No, no, no. That isn't how I want to respond. I want to work on this. I guess I'll take a few breaths before responding.*

Having a one-word reminder allowed Elliot to zoom out enough to get curious about their own response and interact with their defensive part rather than respond from it. Elliot was then able to respond to Rachel more calmly, letting her know that they are taking a few breaths and will be home soon. Without this cue word, Elliot could have easily been consumed by their defensive part and the interaction could have escalated to a blowout fight. But because Rachel and Elliot have been working on noticing their individual parts, Rachel was able to use their cue word to prompt Elliot to take a step back. This can also work in person, when one partner takes a deep breath and prompts the other with a cue word after recognizing that the partner is getting heated and having a parts-based response.

Example 2:

Stephen and Drew have been working on their communication and trying not to interact from a parts-based response. They have developed the cue word "story" to remind themselves to get curious about the story they are telling themselves that is causing a protective part to respond and take a moment to find themselves through curiosity.

One night, Stephen makes an elaborate dinner to celebrate Drew's big promotion, but he does not tell Drew about his plans. He spends all afternoon running around making the preparations in anticipation of Drew's arrival. Five minutes before Drew is expected to arrive home, Stephen texts him to ask when he plans to be home. Drew, having no knowledge of Stephen's plans, stopped at the store after work to buy supplies for a project he wanted to work on that night. Consumed in his planning, Drew leaves his phone in the car and misses Stephen's call. Stephen becomes anxious about his plan falling through and repeatedly calls Drew. He finally becomes irritated and sends Drew a clipped message questioning his whereabouts. Drew returns to his phone to find several missed calls and an angry text from Stephen. Confused, Drew calls Stephen, who is very short in his responses, and the conversation ends quickly. Drew sends a follow-up message using their cue word "story."

Stephen can respond in one of two ways:

1) Stephen's angry part response/internal dialogue:
   Story? I'm not telling myself a story. My feelings are real! I made this elaborate plan to celebrate Drew, and he didn't even have the decency to tell me he planned to go to the

store or ask if it was an inconvenience. *He can be so selfish. Ugh! I'm just going to throw all this away! Drew can celebrate by himself tonight! I'm not even going to respond. That will show him!*

2) Stephen's curious response/internal dialogue:
Story? Well, that's annoying. I feel really angry. I want to give Drew a piece of my mind and forget this whole night. I could do that, but he did just use the cue word, so can I get curious about what I'm feeling? Why am I feeling this way? What's this part of me really upset about?

Choosing the curious response allows Stephen to take the time and space he needs to shift out of anger and toward compassion. Curiosity allows him the space to choose his response. Stephen's internal dialogue:

I'm angry because I put a lot of time and effort into this surprise and we weren't on the same page. That's really frustrating. I'm not wrong for feeling frustrated. Did Drew know that I was planning this for him? No, he didn't. Would he have gone to the store if he had known? Probably not. Is it fair for me to take my frustration out on him and ruin this night for both of us? No, it wouldn't be fair to him, and it wouldn't be fair to me either. The food can be reheated, and we can still connect and celebrate.

Of course, it is not always as easy or simple as these examples. Learning to get curious about our responses and emotions takes time and practice, but it does get easier. We *can* learn to notice our emotions and response urges before acting on them. We *can* learn to give ourselves the validation and compassion we deserve, like

Stephen did in recognizing that his situation really was frustrating and his feelings were valid. It makes sense that these concepts seem foreign and overwhelming because, unfortunately, many of us were not taught how to identify our feelings, nor had our feelings validated. Without being taught these basic skills, how could we know how to do this for ourselves? Before getting down on yourself or writing this off as too difficult to comprehend, send yourself some compassion, acknowledge how difficult it is to learn a new skill and change old patterns, and get curious about any resistance you may be feeling.

From a Queer Lens

For members of the queer community, it is very common to have a protective part that rejects some element of that queer identity. Remember, those childlike parts are big hurts, attachment wounds, shame, sadness, and fear of rejection. And the protector parts are then managing the situation or our reactions in an effort to keep us from feeling that shame, pain, and rejection. So, it stands to reason that queer individuals, knowing society's inherent rejection and having lived experiences of rejection, abuse, and/or microaggressions, will likely have a protector part that is present during both the identification and development of their queer identity, as well as throughout the coming out process. Sometimes this protector is so strong that it actually inhibits the coming out process altogether. Other times, it shows up in the form of self-loathing, shame, or situational rejection, which again, is just a protector trying to keep us from feeling pain. The protector's logic is that if we hate or internally reject our identity enough, it will keep us safe from feeling pain; it will keep us safe from being rejected; it will keep us safe from society's hatred.

The clinical work I do with these individuals is parallel to the work I do with individuals who do not identify as queer, but with an added dimension of **intersectional identity**. This means we identify the protectors that are in place, determine what they are trying to protect and what they are afraid of, and then reparent that tiny, childlike part that is afraid of rejection. We do this by reassuring that part of each individual that their adult self would never reject them, but instead embrace them fully and with genuine authenticity.

This is not to say that even through the reparenting we will not have times of concern or fear of safety over our identity, just that it will not be a reaction that is part-based, but is more of a compassionate curiosity toward the world and ourselves. Remember Hannah, whose mother rejected her so frequently that she learned to push away and hate aspects of herself (including her budding queer identity)? We would work together to help Hannah acknowledge, greet, and extend loving energy to all parts of herself in an effort to validate her experience and help her grow closer to her full, authentic self.

What If I Can't Find My "Self"?

Sometimes, when we have had so many different or compounded traumas, we develop multiple layers of protectors and childlike parts. It can be frustrating to try to sift through all those reactions and responses, and at times, different protectors will really dig in because they have had to throughout our history. In moments like these, the desperation and urgency are very real, and we can feel like we are just a compilation of rapidly switching parts. So, instead of becoming frustrated trying to locate our "Self," we need to extend ourselves some grace and locate the most adult-like part we can to assist us in the situation at hand. This might be a manager part that takes over when life feels really overwhelming—we cannot juggle everything, we are on the verge of a meltdown, the kids are screaming, the dogs are barking, and the doorbell is ringing. While it would be ideal to be able to transcend all that, take a deep breath, and find our center, sometimes that is just not realistic in the moment.

Remember, this is a *process*. It is unlikely that you will be able to locate that elusive "Self" right off the bat, especially with a long and compounded trauma history. The first step is regulating the situation and yourself. Manage the chaos at hand before dinner burns on the stove, then, after the pandemonium has quelled, try to look back and be curious about what was going on in that situation that made things feel so unmanageable. Regulation and curiosity are keys to beginning this journey!

Disclaimer

The next chapter explicitly focuses on explicit experiences of trauma. It can be very beneficial to read for partners who are trying to support individuals who have gone through these types of experiences and can be validating to individuals who experienced it themselves. However, it could also be very triggering or activating to read for a part or parts of you. Please take a moment to check in with your parts and help compassionately prepare them for the content ahead.

Ask yourself what it is you are feeling in this moment.

Notice how this feeling may be tied to any sensations in your body.

Now, ask yourself what this feeling is trying to tell you. Is there a part of you who feels worried about what you might read and how that might make you feel? Is there a part of you who feels annoyed with this check-in and would rather ignore any anxiety and press onward?

Take a moment to send acknowledgement to any parts you may be noticing. Let them know that you see them, their concerns are valid, and they are being taken seriously. To the anxious part, you may say, "I hear that you're worried about being triggered by whatever may be in this chapter. It makes sense that you wouldn't want to feel distressed. Thank you for looking out for me." To the part who is annoyed by this exercise, you may say, "I hear that you find this exercise frustrating and/or annoying. It makes sense that you want to be able to read a book without having to pause and do check-ins."

Send out a general broadcast to all the parts, reminding them of their ability to speak up at any time. If the material becomes too much, if you begin to feel distressed or overwhelmed, your parts are welcome to ask you to take a break and check in. These parts may communicate this to you in the form of suddenly feeling tired or a having a fogginess settle in your forehead. They may alert you through a tightening in your chest or an increase of your heart rate. Keep a lookout for these signs of communication from your parts as you read on, because they may be trying to ask you to slow down, take a break, or skip over this section completely. This work is all about learning to listen to ourselves and what it is we might be needing moment to moment.

Chapter 4
The Type of Trauma Matters

I carry my roots with me all the time /
Rolled up, I use them as my pillow.
— Francisco X. Alarcón

The type of trauma we come into a relationship with matters. Because experience with trauma inlays the way we think about ourselves and the world, exactly *when* we experienced this trauma impacts the downstream fallout. For example, if an individual experiences emotional abuse at the age of six, during which time their father consistently tells them that they are "worthless" and/ or is overtly critical and regularly states that they "will never be good enough," that individual's confidence in themself, their belief in the possibility of success, and their self-esteem in general will be pushed off balance. Their foundational beliefs about themself experience an oil spill of vitriol on the river of who they are. This oil spill impacts everything downstream—everything they experience—and the way they look at themself and the world is seen through a sludgy film.

In response to this oil spill, the body and brain try to make meaning of these messages, which is a natural adaptation to the new "poison." As children, we are biologically programmed to trust in our caregivers, so when they tell us things—even vile and hateful things—we believe them. We believe that they know better because they are adults. Once this happens, our brains start collecting that "evidence" into our memory "folders," each labeled with a cognition or belief about ourselves. We begin to collect, prove, verify, and validate those thoughts until the message "I'm not good enough" fortifies itself. It can show up when we don't make the T-ball team, when we get turned down when asking out a love interest, or when we get passed over for a promotion. Over time, these small file folders turn into huge storage units of "proof"—a lifetime of evidence that, without that initial trauma, might have been stored away under "unfortunate circumstance" or "a bummer of a situation."

These seminal events of trauma that happen in childhood therefore send our trajectory of self-worth and self-esteem off course very early on in our development, turning a single incident oil spill into a plume of toxic fallout. If there is ongoing or complex trauma, there are multiple spills that only further complicate our internal ecosystems. Everything downstream gets stuck to and intertwined with the negative beliefs and messages.

Interpersonal trauma in adulthood can have similar impact, it just starts a little further down the road. For example, if someone's first romantic relationship at age 18 results in their seemingly loving boyfriend forcing himself upon them, that person's brain starts a file folder related to romantic relationships and their worth and safety within them. They may develop new beliefs around the words "love," "sex," "connection," and/or "vulnerability." Their actions in future relationships will be impacted by this experience, and any further relational issues (even things that might otherwise be over-looked) will be filed in their newly minted file folder.

The two case studies coming up illustrate a deeper look into developmental trauma and adult interpersonal trauma. I chose to focus specifically on these two because they are the most common experiences I see in relationship counseling, and the impact of these traumas can be vastly different and show up in many ways. There are, of course, several other types of trauma, but common themes I see more frequently than not (e.g., betrayal, lack of safety, skewed sense of self concept), show up in many of them, so there are some relational similarities in how they present in relationships.

Nora's story is a compilation of information I have seen, worked with, and studied, and Jen's story is inspired from elements of my personal survival story. Many things have been written about domestic violence, varying from why perpetrators do it to why victims stay. I cannot speak for the general populace, but I can speak for myself. In telling a bit of my story, I hope to help shed some light on the possibilities of different dynamics and parts that can exist in a relationship that contains domestic violence. To assist with immersion into the full experience from the trauma event to takeaways, both stories are written in first person.

Developmental Trauma Case Example: Nora

The smell of cigars and Old Spice. The darkness of the wood-paneled walls of the recessed basement. The stack of dog-eared children's books and dirty doll faces, one with an eye that wouldn't close all the way. Mirrored beer signs and an old slot machine that only took pennies. The feeling of warm urine running down my leg when I hear the crack of the beer can as his footsteps come down the stairs. Lately, his voice sounds different when he calls my name. There's a deepness to it; a whisper laced with desperation. It only happens when Mommy's gone. At first, I was excited when she got the new job in the city because it meant that I could get a new bike and some of the new books I wanted (instead of having to read the books from the library that smell funny and are always missing a few pages). It also meant I would get to spend more time with Daddy. He used to work nights and I didn't see him much. When I did, it was when I'd sneak down to his basement and sit with him while he watched baseball on Saturday afternoons. Then he lost his job, and Mommy started working overnights as a nurse at a hospital 45 minutes away.

One Saturday when I'm eight, Mommy heads to work and Daddy retreats to his basement to watch the Tigers versus the Kansas City Royals. I make my way down the steps and plop down on a cushion beside his recliner.

"Hey, kid! Grab me another beer from the kegerator, will ya?"

I spring up and race over to the bar area, previously unknown and off-limits territory. I pull open the little brown door and pull out a Budweiser. It's a warm one out today, so the cold can feels good on my hot hands. I bring it back to Daddy and return to my cushion. The game plays on and every so often, Daddy tasks me with another beer run. This time when I come back, his hand brushes against mine when I hand over the can.

"Whoa! You're freezing! Come here and let your old man steal some of that chill; it's roasting down here!"

He pulls me onto his lap, pressing my hand against his cheek and the back of his neck. His skin is so warm and sticky with sweat, and his breath is thick with alcohol. He playfully hoists me off his lap and with a twinkle in his eye, asks me to get two more cans from the bar, one for each of us!

Pulling me back onto his lap when I return, he presses one can to the back of his neck and instructs me to do the same. The can is freezing on my neck! We both laugh and squirm, trying to press the cold cans against one another to see who whoops the loudest.

The laughter dies down, and Daddy chuckles to himself, "Well, look at that, isn't that cute?" as he's staring at my chest.

My eight-year-old nipples are hard and pointy. Daddy slowly runs a cold can down the front of my shirt, watching my nipples harden. Again. And again. Then he leans down and uses his breath to warm them, only to run the can down again. It tickles and I laugh and squirm. His eyes change, his breathing becomes ragged, and I can feel his heart pounding in his chest.

Licking his lips and then wiping his hand down the length of his face, he clears his throat and says, "Alright, kiddo, let's go make dinner."

He playfully lifts me off his lap and ruffles my hair. *This is the most fun with Daddy I've ever had! I never knew he was so silly!*

A few weeks later, Daddy invites me to go fishing with him. He never does that! I'm so excited! I throw on my new jelly sandals and race him to the truck. He throws the rods and the cooler in the back, and we climb in the single cab pickup. Playfully flopping his hat on my head, he says, "Ready to go, copilot?" *Copilot? I've never been Daddy's copilot before!* He starts the truck, and we head down the road to the pond a few miles away.

When we get there, I spring out of the truck and run down to the water's edge. Daddy grabs the poles, the cooler, and a dusty old blanket from the bed of the truck. "I thought we might have a little picnic today."

OMG, this is the funnest day ever!

Daddy baits his hook and casts it expertly into the middle of the pond before sticking the pole in the sand and watching the bobber float on the glass surface of the water. He spreads out the blanket on the bank, takes a beer from the cooler, and plops down, stretching his legs and lifting his face toward the sun. "Come 'ere, squirt," he calls to me, patting a spot on the blanket.

I amble over and take my coveted place next to him. *He's the best dad ever. How did I never notice how cool he was?!*

As the day lazily moves on, Daddy dips back into the cooler several times. "Hey, wanna see something neat?" he asks.

"Heck yes!" I reply.

"Remember when we were playing in the basement the other day?"

Duh! So fun!

Running a cold can over my nipples, he continues, "You know how when I did this, that happened?"

I laugh. *Daddy's so silly!*

He scoots closer to me saying, "You know, you can also make that happen like this," as he runs the back of his hand across my chest, gently pinching my nipple between his pointer and middle fingers. It tingles and tickles at the same time. Daddy's eyes are doing that thing again.

"Want to know something else, baby girl? Sometimes when there's someone very special, they have superpowers. They can touch someone and make something like that happen on other parts of their body."

"No way!" I blurt out. "That's craziness! What a cool power to have control over other people's bodies! That's almost as good as mind control!"

"Can I show you?" Daddy asks.

"Yes, show me, Daddy!" I exclaim. *I wonder if I'm one of those special people that has a special power!*

Daddy takes my hand and places it on his inner thigh. He starts breathing funny again. He moves my hand up higher toward his "private area."

"Daddy," I nervously chuckle and instinctively try to pull my hand away, "that's a private area."

He holds my wrist tighter. *How is he so strong?* I feel something on his body shift, move, harden.

Daddy sighs and closes his eyes. "Look, baby girl, you have the special power," he says as he breathes heavier and moves my hand all around. He says things he's never said before, like "You are so special," "You're Daddy's good girl," and "No one makes me happy like you do."

I love Daddy and am so excited to have a special power! I'm also confused and a little embarrassed.

We come back to the lake almost every day. Daddy helps me learn all about my special power, and we practice all the time! Sometimes he does it for me, and sometimes he even lets me do it all by myself. He says that if I keep practicing, I'll be able to learn even more superpowers.

After a few weeks, Daddy tries to teach me a new power. It hurts! I'd rather use my hands, but he says that this way is better. It's scary and I feel like I'm going to rip in two. I ask Daddy to stop, but he tells me that this is how people show love and that he's never loved someone as much as me. *I'm special.* Daddy says that I can't tell anyone, though, because people wouldn't understand our love. *I want to keep feeling special. I want Daddy to keep loving me. I'm afraid he'll be mad if I ask him to stop. But it hurts. Sometimes it feels good too. This must be what love feels like.* Sometimes Daddy says nice things. Sometimes he just grunts. Sometimes all I hear is static.

One day, it started to hurt when I pee. I tried to wash extra good in the tub, but the next day, it was burning like fire! I tell my mom. She's a nurse and says it's likely a UTI, so she takes me to the doctor's office. I sit on the paper-covered table while Mommy talks on the phone to her sister about work and money. Boring stuff. I pick at the corner of the paper. I like the way I can rip off pieces and roll them into little balls.

The doctor comes in. He's older than me but younger than Daddy. He asks me all sorts of questions. He has a nice smile. Inviting me to lie back on the table, he starts pushing on my belly, asking me if it hurts. He must have the superpower too! His hands are cold. I take one of his hands and swiftly guide it under my shirt, mimicking a moan. His startled hand grazes my breast. Everything happens in slow motion. His eyes bug. He rips his hand away from mine. Mommy drops the phone and opens her mouth to yell. All I hear is static. I'm wearing my jelly sandals again.

On the way home, Mommy asks a million questions. I don't want to lie to her, because she's my mom! But she seems really mad. I don't want her to be mad at Daddy. I just shrug my shoulders and lean my head against the cool window. *Daddy told me that if I ever told Mommy, she'd send him away and I'd never see him again.*

Mommy storms into the house and starts yelling at Daddy. Daddy looks surprised. Then he looks mad. He's yelling back at her. All I hear are muffled voices. Daddy's telling Mommy that he didn't do anything and that maybe it was just something I saw on TV. He must want to keep our superpowers a secret. Lying to Mommy seems wrong, though. All of a sudden, I can't breathe. My heartbeat is in my ears. Everything's going black. My legs give out.

I wake up and Daddy is wiping my face with a cool cloth. I'm in my bed. Daddy whispers that we can't tell Mommy anything.

"It seems wrong to lie to Mommy," I say.

Daddy's face gets mad. So mad. His eyes squint and redness creeps up his neck. His nostrils flare and his jaw sets. His voice changes again, but this time it's cold.

Daddy starts coming into my room at night. He's not silly any- more. He seems mad. He's rough. I try doing everything to get silly

Daddy back again. Sometimes it works and he says nice things like "You're special" and "I love you more than anyone." Sometimes he's mean and threatening, though. He says he'll hurt Mommy if I tell anyone. Sometimes he cries. *I know I can cheer him up. I'm his special girl.*

Daddy stops when I get my period at age 11. He never calls me his special girl anymore. He doesn't invite me to go fishing. *What did I do to be rejected so significantly?! The relationship we had was special. I feel so lost. I feel so alone. So empty. I want to feel love again.*

I feel love again with the neighbor boy who is two years older than me. I show him my superpowers and he seems to like it. I feel less empty.

I feel empty again. I feel like I'm drowning. I can't breathe. I start cutting myself; it's a rush of excitement and then calm. It's kinda like love, right? Sometimes cutting doesn't help, though. The noise is too loud. The pain is too unbearable. The numbness, emptiness, and heaviness are too much. I start drinking and smoking pot when I'm too jacked to stop my hands from shaking. I barter bathroom blowjobs for Ritalin so I can bring my head above water when I'm too empty to function. I don't know what love is. I don't know what hate is. All I know is I feel nothing and everything at the same time. I don't know what's real or what's safe. I don't know what trust is. Who am I? Where does my body end and the needs/wants of others begin?

Nora's Takeaways

My internal house is built on love made of poison and safety made of lies. Every board is filled with termites, every thought about myself is skewed, every belief I have about the world is fucked. All I have are folders full of fake narratives—fantasies and fairy tales and nightmarish horror stories.

This type of developmental trauma is impacting not only my idea of who I am, my worth as a person, and my belief (or disbelief) in my autonomy, but also my conceptions about my role in the lives of others. When entering into new relationships, I have a tendency to try to please my partner immediately. This allows me to have some sort of control over the safety of the situation so that I feel like I'm protected. I also lose myself and my identity in relationships, often taking on the likes and dislikes of my partner, pushing my limits, and not speaking up when my boundaries are crossed. This proactive manager part steps in and has a fawning response to my partner, even when my partner is supportive and kind.

I know these are my survival responses and part reactions. My attachment to a primary figure in my life created the blueprint on which my beliefs of myself are built. Because this trauma happened so early in my development, I had little outside reference or influence with which to combat these messages and instead had to use the information that was presented to me, which was incredibly damaging.

Sometimes I feel deeply for my partner, and it scares me. As soon as I feel the intense love and connection, I immediately think of all the ways I could lose them or all the things I could do wrong that might push them away. Sometimes that makes me run away or disengage because I'm so sure I'm going to fail. Then they get upset and call me on it, which makes me feel ashamed and validates my fear that I'm going to mess something up. I feel like I'm not worthy of love or that I might never be able to love the way I feel like I should. Sometimes I feel too broken to see any light. Even though I never feel it's possible, I desperately want to belong. This disruption of my sense of self is a common CPTSD symptom related to relational disruption.

I have parts that are very entrenched and have been active for such a long time that it's difficult for me *not* to function as a con-glomeration of parts. Sometimes, instead of being able to find my inner adult-functioning parts or transcendent energy, I bounce from part response to part response, never fully staying in my window of tolerance or being able to fully remain in a social connection vagal state.

In relationships, I need a partner who can understand that I'm sometimes my own worst enemy and encourage me to be my own best friend. This isn't an easy task, because I typically think more highly of others than myself. My disorganized attachment means that sometimes I can be very reactive or not reactive at all, and I know that's frustrating for a partner. It's really hard for me too.

Adult Interpersonal Trauma Case Example: Jen

I met him during a transitional time in my life, when I was getting out of one relationship and treading water until I went back to col-lege. As with most great mistakes, I went in blindly. At first, it was magical. He made me feel loved, cherished, like the center of his universe. Having just gotten out of a relationship in which I felt less than, like a second choice or fallback option, I felt like being some-one else's gravity was appealing. Intoxicating.

Things progressed quickly with this new beau, and we moved in together within the first three months. At first it was us "playing house." We felt like we were on our own individual planet of passion and love, of laughter and inside jokes. The summer flew by, and as the leaves turned, so did the temperature of our relationship. I started back to school, which meant I had to be away from home more frequently. Late nights, study groups, internships, new friends… all things that should be exciting. But instead, this transition bred jealousy, suspicion, fear, and anxiety. It started slowly, with suspicious asking of questions about where I was and who I was with. I would reassure him, and his anger would quickly melt away and be replaced with kisses.

As the days and weeks went on, the suspicions grew stronger and the kisses grew less frequent. Instead of smiles, it was slammed doors. Instead of flowers, it was screaming. Suspicions then led to accusations. He would assume that I had been out late because I was dating someone else, assume that friends were lovers, assume that phone calls and text messages were of a nefarious nature. My queerness became a weapon—there are twice as many possible affairs when you are bisexual, so I was often accused of flirting with literally everyone. He would also sometimes say things like, "Don't act so gay!" which became my internal messages of, *Be overtly touchy toward him in public. Ignore individuals of the same sex.*

I pulled away from friends and family because I did not want to upset him. This came in such an organic way that it seemed like my idea. It was scary how much I wanted to make him happy and how easily and quickly it happened. He would pout, and I would say no to invitations for coffee with friends. He would purposefully plan romantic dinners—special date nights—during my scheduled study groups or during times I was supposed to work or be in class. To him, having outside obligations was me "not prioritizing our relationship." *Make sure he knows you love him. Tell him. Tell him again.*

Soon, I was making excuses as to why I could not see family. I tried to push back at times, but that would lead to him yelling, crying, or making statements about "not knowing if the relationship was going to work if I wasn't going to put in the effort." I would end up holding him and reassuring him that he was important—and canceling any plans I had. At this point, I was still so in love, still living on that island with him. I still saw flashes of goodness in him, and there were still times when he could make me feel so special. But our home had started to lose its sparkle. The light was leaving, and it was becoming a prison—a prison with an unknowing captive.

It was an open-handed slap across the face. One slap that began months of increasing physical, emotional, and sexual abuse. He had issues with alcohol prior to this, and those only intensified. The paranoia, accusations, and violence went hand in hand. It would start with his increasing panic and anxiety about my whereabouts, compounded by his being drowned in a pint of tequila or vodka that he followed up with shoves against the wall or slaps to my face, and finished off with a chaser of his favorite beverage. Then he would be wracked with shame and guilt, apologizing, buying gifts, trying to right the wrong. Until the next study group. Rinse and repeat. Rinse and repeat. *Don't make excuses, just agree. Don't make him mad.*

I started having panic attacks 15 minutes before returning home, dreading the thought of climbing the stairs and walking through the door. Was I going to be met with flowers or fists? *What does his face say? How does the air feel? What is the energy like?* I became so codependently attuned to his every mood, any twitch in his face, any clenching of his jaw, any flicker of his eyes. And in response, I would fawn any possible trigger for his anger. I believed that if I could work out the mental chess game, I could keep him from exploding and would have my loving boyfriend back. *It's my fault he's mad. It's my fault I'm getting hurt.*

I continued attending grad school and then coming home to him. Going to grad school for social work, I was taking a freaking class on domestic violence and was still coming home to him. As my awareness increased, there were times when I wanted to get out, wanted to run. I was mad at myself for staying, and I was mad at myself for considering leaving. This was still the man who made me feel special, the man who carried in his hands the ability to make me feel like the center of the universe. *If you want to feel special, go along with whatever he says.* This internal conflict sometimes led to confrontation. At times, I would even pack a bag, but then he would cry, berate himself for what he had done, and shame himself for using violence. He would make promises that it would never happen again and sometimes even threatened to kill himself. I would stay because, after all, I loved him. I did not want to be the cause of his pain and definitely not the cause of his suicide. *You're responsible for his happiness. You're responsible for his safety. You can't advocate for yourself. You need to just shut up.*

Through all of it, I saw the different parts of him: the anxious and scared little boy that was afraid I was going to leave, the small child who never thought he was good enough, the man who still couldn't make his father happy even though he had grown up, and the son who knew he was not his mother's favorite. I could see all these parts and all the reasons why his life had led him to this. I could see the pain, the anger, and the sadness. I could also see the smashing of glass as he threw his cup across the living room. The rage in his eyes. *Placate to protect myself.*

At that time, the action was negated because of the explanation. I could see why he did it, and it made me care about that little boy inside. So, I stayed. *Forgive him no matter what. He can't help hurting you, but you can control how many excuses you give him to do so.*

I stayed when he put his hands around my throat and demanded that I tell him I was sleeping with a professor (I was not).

I stayed when he knocked me out before a final exam in hopes I would fail out of college.

I stayed when he made me clean the bathroom for three hours, naked, because I was a "dirty whore who tainted everything with my filth."

I stayed when he ignored my "no's" and "stop's."

And I stayed when he drunkenly held a gun to my head and made me promise never to leave.

I stayed.

You know you can't do anything right? So stop trying to convince him you're right. Maybe you're not right. Maybe he's always right. Maybe you did flirt with that waiter. Maybe you did ignore his phone call. Maybe you did lie about your whereabouts.

The things he would tell me that related to who I was as a person started becoming my inner self-worth. He would tell me that no one would want me after all that had happened, so I might as well stay with him because I was ruined. In the same breath he used to beg me to stay, he would tell me that I was disgusting, unlovable, a whore, while his eyes would change from pleading to cold. *I'm not worthy of love or safety.* I could see the different parts of him fighting to maintain control by any means necessary: begging, crying, threatening, hurting, forcing, anger, control, anxiety, shame, more anger, more control. *Giving up control is the only way to survive.*

My safe and loving family would have scooped me up in a heartbeat. They never would have allowed me to stay in that situation if they had known. But I was so ashamed of what was happening, of who I had become, and of what I thought I had let happen to me—I couldn't face them. The person they knew was so far from the person I had become.

Eventually, I started to pull away. I could not ignore the conflicting messages I was getting between my classes at school and the lessons at home. He could feel that, though, and the scared little boy inside who was afraid of being abandoned clung on tighter. *I'm not strong enough to leave. I'm not strong enough to stay.* That is when he started trying to get me pregnant. If we had a child together, I "could never really leave."

When someone is intentionally trying to get you pregnant, they typically don't use condoms, so I used birth control pills and would hide them. It did not matter whether I wanted him or not; he wanted me, and he always got what he wanted. Sometimes, I would not fight, because fighting only hurt more. But I never gave consent. *Close your eyes and go away. Fighting back means more pain.* Sometimes he would find my birth control, flush it down the toilet, punish me for lying to him, and then wash down his sins with a bottle of vodka.

Eventually, a friend found out what was happening one afternoon when my bruises were too visible to hide. She offered to help in any way possible. Though I was not ready to leave yet, I asked her to keep my pills at her house so he could not find them. I successfully evaded pregnancy.

The more time I spent at my internship and in class, the more I was able to pull away long enough to come up for air. I finally came to the realization that if I did not get out of this situation, it was not going to end well for me. The violence and paranoia kept increasing. His fear of losing me kept intensifying. When he did reach out to me, it was either in anger or lust, as if he were trying to reclaim me and force me back into the person I was when we first met. He wanted me to look at him with love, passion, and trust. Anything else was me pulling away from him. But trust comes with safety, and that was long gone. *Your boundaries don't matter. The only way to stay alive is to make him happy. Don't pull away. Let him reach for you. Let him take you. Let him…*

Reaching out to family in the area, I was able to find a new place to live, and I slipped away one afternoon while he was at work. He followed me, frequently begging or intimidating me and cycling through the little children inside of him. The scared boy in fear of abandonment, the angry child who will never be enough, each threatening me, each throwing their fists in the air, each stomping their feet in panic-fueled hatred.

But I stayed away.

He threatened to kill me.

I stayed away.

He tried to commit suicide, taking pictures of knives, blood, and his tear-streaked face as step-by-step memoirs of what I had done to him and sending them to me in ever-intensifying succession. Then silence. No texts for two hours. My heart ached for him. Panicked for him. My guilt. My shame. *My fault.* His family did not know what he had been doing to me, so they called me incessantly from the ER while his wrist was getting glued, their anger for my seemingly unwarranted "abandonment" of their son/brother echoing in the chambers of my voicemail box.

I stayed away.

He waited outside of my school and assaulted me in a parking garage three blocks from the university, the structure's "Red Level 2" sign burning in my brain forever, along with its chipping paint and smell of exhaust.

I stayed quiet. I stayed alive.

I stayed away.

He threatened that if I did not come back to him, this would continue to happen forever.

I stayed away.

I never told anyone what happened, aside from the few friends who found out and the family who let me move in. For years to come, I kept it to myself. The trauma created shame in me, making me think it was my fault and training me to believe that he was doing those things because he loved me or because I was inherently bad. He made me feel like I did not deserve love, safety, or joy.

Even though I stayed away, these messages continued to permeate my life over the next several years, weaseling their way into my relationships with friends, family, and partners. I could see these messages—his beliefs—had now become my own. My actions echoed these beliefs, so I would sabotage relationships because I never felt good enough. I would choose people I knew were not the right choice because I thought I did not deserve any better. I would put up with things that I never put up with before because I was counting my lucky stars that someone, anyone, wanted to be with me. His words still echo in my head. For a long time, I was afraid of drawing any attention to myself because I had hidden for so long. I had hidden my face, my bruises, my shame.

When I came out publicly as bisexual, it was at great protest to many of my inner parts who did not want to be seen, and I definitely did not want to be defined by anything related to my sexuality. He had made so much of my sexual experiences negative: sex equals pain; love equals shame. He would claim that I could only be "him-sexual"—only be attracted to him—and through creative and disgusting means would make sure I would never forget that. So, it was beyond painful to not only come out, but to justify my sexuality in ways I had previously hidden. And it didn't help knowing that some members of society would have stronger opinions about what went on behind the closed doors of my bedroom with a woman than about what had happened behind closed doors with him.

Jen's Takeaways

These burdens or beliefs that I was not good enough, and the actions I needed to take to be safe, were partnered with parts of myself who would step in to protect me internally. One part of me would feel like I should apologize profusely when my partner was critical of me, and another would want to stand up and say, "No way! I don't have to listen to you!" The latter part—the advocate—was silenced, pushed down as a means of survival, because it was not safe to advocate for myself. Similarly, since mothers typically get the bulk of their child's misbehavior, because children feel safe and comfortable enough to be any and all versions of themselves, loving and safe relationships can also be ground zero for parts that need to be heard and now have the safety to do so.

My current relationship is loving and safe, and because of that, my advocate part no longer has to be silent. It can appear during times of proportionate need (e.g., when I am not feeling heard or important), as well as during times when there is a disproportionate trigger (e.g., when I really don't want to unload the dishwasher). However, this advocate part cannot typically differentiate the degree of need or intensity, only that it *is* needed. And since it has the safety and space to be vocal, it will be.

My wife might ask, for example, "Hey, I saw the cleaning supplies out. Did you clean the bathroom?" While normally this would be a pretty innocuous question, given my trauma history with a man who made me clean the bathrooms for hours while insisting they were never clean enough and possibly becoming physically violent, this question could seem like a criticism of the quality of my cleanliness. My internal dialogue might look like this: *Oh, no! I must've missed something. If she can't tell I already cleaned, it must be disgusting in there! I need to apologize, drop everything, and clean it again. I can't believe I didn't do a better job. Stupid, stupid, stupid! I'm so worthless! She's going to leave me. I just know it! What kind of person can't even clean a bathroom?!* The appearance of this reaction would subsequently trigger the advocate part of me to swoop in and protect this shame reaction. This might look like the response my wife would get from me: "Of course I did! Can't you tell? What the hell, babe?!

I work my butt off all day and make sure I do extra stuff like cook dinner, pick up the kids, and, yes, clean the bathroom, and the first thing you do when you get home is criticize?! Why am I working so hard if you don't even notice?!"

Vocal parts of us are not necessarily indicative of significant problems in a relationship dynamic, but instead might be an indicator that we feel safe enough to feel and express all parts. While this freedom of expression might not feel so great in the moment, it does provide us with insight into what our triggers are, what we need to feel safe, and how we can work on communicating those things in a way that is both authentic and helpful.

Thankfully, a scenario like this would now be met with, "Babe [insert "patient-knowing-but-still-not-okay-to-snap-at-me" look here]," followed by a moment of reflection, a deep breath, and calling myself out: "Aw, shit. I'm sorry."

Through similar work, we can each learn to reassure our protector parts that they don't need to be so vehement in their protection and our hurt parts that our environment is safe and loving and there is always room to grow.

Digging Deeper: Explore Your "File Folders"

First, take a moment to do some grounding work: take some deep breaths, go for a walk, cook a meal, connect with a supportive person, or laugh at a "dad joke." Recognize any parts that may need a little extra attention or reassurance, and validate any parts that may have had a difficult time with the content of this chapter.

Next, if you feel up to it, read back over the first section of this chapter. Then, write about the "file folders" of negative core beliefs you have. While doing so, think about your answers to these questions:

- What are those core beliefs about yourself that inform your daily life?
- Where did they come from?
- How have they impacted your decisions about yourself and your relationships?
- Can you challenge those negative beliefs?
- What is some "evidence" that conflicts with those?

Example:
Amy has a file folder of "I'm not loveable" after her mother's repeated verbal abuse. This caused Amy to push away from any equitable romantic relationships and omit boundaries from friendships. She does not demand or expect to be treated well in relationships; in fact, at times she feels deeply uncomfortable with expressions of love, as they feel disingenuous.

She feels that she should take what she can get in relationships and therefore tends to attract individuals who exploit her emotional generosity and lack of boundaries.

Explore Your Own:

_____

_____

_____

_____

_____

_____

_____

_____

_____

_____

_____

_____

_____

_____

_____

_____

Part 2

The "So What?" of "Our Stuff"

Chapter 5
Common Relational Issues

In a forest of a hundred thousand trees,
no two leaves are alike.
And no two journeys along the same path are alike.
— Paulo Coelho

Within the last few chapters, we unpacked various ways that we individually experience and process trauma. We looked at ways that we internalize messages of safety and worth and have started to identify and label our own attachment structures and styles. In this chapter, we will discuss different relational dynamics and dances that happen when two or more people with a trauma history come together in a romantic relationship. By exploring attachment and power dynamics, we will begin to shift our focus from what is going on inside of us to what is going on inside our relationships. From there, we begin the discussion of why we have that same fight over and over again and how we can stop pissing each other off and hurting each other's feelings.

Attachment Needs of You and Your Partner(s)

Throughout my experience counseling individuals and couples, I have frequently seen pairings that include a partner who has an anxious attachment style and a partner who has either an avoidant or disorganized attachment style. This pairing makes sense! The anxiously attached partner's parts see opportunities for connection and helping, while the avoidant (or disorganized) partner's parts see opportunities for intense and intermittent connection anytime they feel the need, with the ability to pull away as needed without fear of losing the relationship. However, as we discussed, anxiously attached individuals often fall into a pattern of fawning, giving in to their partners to avoid a fight, rejection, or anything that could upset the relationship. In their past, this anxiously attached individual did not know when or if they would get their needs met, so they clung to any opportunity for affection or love by frantically trying to prevent or fix any situation that could lead to rejection. Avoidantly attached individuals are just that—avoidant. It was not safe for them to have needs when they were younger because those needs were unlikely to get met, so they learned not to depend on anyone. When things get too intense, they are likely to push away.

When one partner in a relationship will try anything to avoid being pushed away and another will pull away at the inclination of vulnerability, it can lead to some intense and immediate power dynamics and disparities in the relationship. Though anxiously attached and avoidantly attached individuals have a common basis for intense attachment or rejection, they respond in many different ways when their parts get involved. When this dance occurs, we might ask ourselves why our partners do what they do.

When Partners Have Anxious Attachment

Why do anxiously attached partners have parts that blame, lecture, seem to only focus on the negative, or set high (and sometimes unrealistic) expectations? Remember, anxious partners had childhoods in which they were shamed, rejected, or ignored.

Example:

Molly's mom was supportive behind closed doors, but would quickly reject Molly when in public. There were many times when Molly's mother would join in on homophobic jokes or comments with her friends. Molly never knew "which mom" would show up. When the supportive version did, Molly wanted to spend as much time with her as possible and trust that maybe this time she would *stay* supportive. Unfortunately, Molly's mom never did, and would just as quickly shift back into rejecting her.

In relationships, Molly has intense feelings of lack of safety when things are awry. This can lead to her blaming, protesting, and lecturing:

If I could just convince you of how you've got it all wrong and you could do it this way, you'd see that I'm right and you'll want to change yourself and then everything will be okay and safe again. You don't seem to be hearing me. Let me use more words, tell you in different ways, tell you in a louder voice. I need to be heard! I never knew when my emotional pain would be responded to in the past, so now I need to be louder and bigger for you to take me seriously and let me know I matter! I might even follow you around the house and demand that we talk about things. Leaving things unresolved is terrifying for me!

You may also see Molly focusing on the negative and having exceedingly high expectations:

I don't trust that I am lovable, so I need you to reassure me and prove to me that you love me and won't abandon me. Even if you reassure me, I don't think I can believe it. I might raise the expectations over and over again, trying to get you to meet that magical place where I *know* you won't leave me. Unfortunately, my past won't let me believe it, even if you don't leave, so I'll have to raise the issue again and again.

Molly can also have a critical part that looks out for potential threats:

If I try to avoid disappointment and always keep a look out for the negative, I won't ever be caught off guard. I should probably point this out to you and tell you what you might be able to do to fix it. If I tell you what you're doing wrong, we can avoid anything painful.

Ultimately, whatever part is speaking for the anxious partner is coming from a place of wanting to get their needs met, even if they are asking in the most frustrating, triggering, and activating ways.

When Partners Have Avoidant Attachment

Avoidant partners came from childhoods in which their caregivers were consistently rejecting and failing to attend to the child's emotional needs. Children in these environments learn that they cannot rely on caregivers for nurturing or safety,[27] so they might proactively fawn as well, but for different reasons. These individuals don't like anything that threatens the relationship homeostasis, especially conflict. Conflict leads to abandonment, and abandonment leads to "proof" that they are "not good enough" or "not worthy of love." You can see this play out in a partner in both proactive and reactive ways. They might try to appease their partner or distract themselves by way of work or substance use.

Example:

George's father rejected him outright when George came out. He would frequently call George names, make comments about him being "a fairy," or just ignore him completely. George learned early on that he could not count on his father to support him in any capacity, simply because he was gay. George's friends also rejected him, ostracizing him from the football team he was captain of and teasing him relentlessly until he quit in his junior year of high school.

Now, George sometimes hides himself or his orientation so that others cannot do the same thing his father and friends did, making it difficult for George to connect and trust that this aspect of himself is not going to push people away:

I'm so afraid of rejection that I need you to see me getting this right. If you're happy, then everything will be okay. I'll do

---

[27] Diane Poole-Heller, *The Power of Attachment: How to Create Deep and Lasting Intimate Relationships* (Boulder, CO: Sounds True, 2019), 57–68.

anything to avoid conflict or feeling bad; I can find all sorts of activities (substance abuse, exercise, working) that make me feel good and successful, unlike relationships that are scary and make me feel vulnerable.

During times of conflict or intense vulnerability, George may freeze or become focused on fixing the issue and move on quickly to avoid spending too much time on it:

Conflict is really overwhelming. I sometimes freeze. I wasn't taught how important feelings are or how to manage them, so it's more comfortable for me to fix them. I might try this technique on you too, because it's all I know. I have a fear of being seen as a failure. If I fail, I'm not "good" and will get rejected. When you tell me something I did wrong, it makes me feel like *I'm* wrong, the way my dad did when I came out to him. How you see me is important, and I can't have you thinking that I'm wrong or bad. Being right means being safe, so I'm going to insist that I'm right and I can't give in. Giving in means I'm a failure and deserve to be abandoned. Bottom line: I hate conflict. Like, a lot. Sometimes it's too painful or scary to sit with it. I'm not running away from you, but from the pain—even if that looks the same. Once I push you away, I might try to get you back, because I really do want to be with you... But am so scared to commit fully.

When Partners Have Disorganized Attachment

For the sake of simplification, disorganized attachment is a combination of anxiously and avoidantly attached characteristics. Individuals with disorganized attachment may vary between desperate desire for attachment and incredible rejection of vulnerability. These partners typically come from homes or relationships that involved elements of terror. In this environment, anything could have happened at any given time, so there was a need to develop numerous ways of coping with the extremes, which may have varied between active abuse to significant emotional neglect (active harm versus intense abandonment).

Example:

Andy's father beat him up the moment he found him kissing his high school best friend, Jason. He was beaten so badly that he had to be hospitalized for two days. At home, his father would often scream at him and try to physically hurt him, and he frequently kicked Andy out of the house, sometimes forcing him to sleep outside or in the barn. Andy's mother left the family when Andy was 16, and Andy's father told Andy it was because "she couldn't handle you being a fag." Most of Andy's parts don't believe this, but some parts are still scared that his dad is right. This history makes it very difficult for Andy to connect with anyone. He is extremely hidden sexually and will react in an explosive way if anyone makes reference to his sexuality. This has caused Andy to lose many friendships and relationships. He desperately wants to connect, but connecting feels so completely unsafe.

Because of Andy's disorganized attachment, he presents very disorganized responses in relationships:

I had to have lots of tools in my toolbox, so I may respond and react in a lot of different ways. These ways may make sense to me, my parts, and my nervous system, but to my partner, they may seem completely out of left field. Often, because of the intensity of my past experiences, a part would step in and take over completely, fully dissociating or shutting off my emotions *or* being completely consumed by them. Now that I'm an adult, this means I'll pull away, shut down, and maybe even stare off into space when I get triggered. Other times, I'll fight with everything I have and say and do things that may be very hurtful. I desperately want connection, but connection and relationships have historically been so confusing and contained so many mixed messages that I don't know how to interpret things at times. And I really don't know how to respond to get my need for connection met.

Andy will often push away and then pull back with equal intensity, viewing his partner as equal extremes of savior and enemy. This can shift quickly with small provocations:

> I'll feel all-consuming love for you, but when I get triggered easily, my brain will make you out to be a very dangerous or hurtful person. It's not responding to you, but to all those people in my past who hurt me so much. Please be patient with me. I'll likely come back to you and be filled with shame at the way I treated you. Sometimes this shame will push me into a self-loathing place, which can cause me to make even worse decisions. I know my unpredictability isn't fair to you. I don't like being this way, it's just all I could do to survive in the past.

As with anxiously attached individuals, individuals with avoidant or disorganized attachment are inherently trying to get their needs met. They are attempting to be in adult relationships and have levels of vulnerability that are needed in these kinds of relationships, but they don't have the blueprints of healthy attachment from childhood or past relationships that would have provided the stability of emotional nurturing. These individuals desire connection, but because their parts don't trust that the connection is safe, those parts will protect the individual through proactive and reactive means. Though this helps keep them safe, it also inhibits true and consistent connection, which in turn inherently impacts both the individual and the relationship. This feedback loop of push-pull, reaction-response can repeat and become entangled with their partner's in such a way that it can impact both partners' ability to build trust and compassion for each other.

Identifying your own attachment style and that of your partner(s) can assist you in knowing how you interact and what steps you can take when those interactions happen. Let's explore other ways partners interact with each other and how you can find connection and compassion.

Reassurance Instead of Rescue or Rejection

With differing attachment styles come differing responses to distress and the distress of our partners. When there is an argument or any large expression of "negative" feelings (e.g., distress, stress, sadness), whether directed at you or not, what is your response? Do you try to move toward your partner to "fix" the situation? Does the established dynamic put you in the position of having to pull your partner out of the "shame spiral" or "pit of despair"? Do you sometimes feel compelled to minimize your needs or feelings, not because your partner is asking you to, but because it makes you so uncomfortable to see your partner in distress? You may be having a "rescue" response.

Rescue

A rescue response can occur when one partner is chronically put in the position to fix their partner's distress and regulate their emotions, either through their partner's expectations or due to their own discomfort with their partner's distress. When this happens, a complicated fallout can result. Since an adult partner's parts have strong distressing emotions that likely come from their younger parts, each person in the relationship should be in individual therapy to work on strengthening their own abilities to meet the needs of their partner's childlike parts. Until that occurs (or if your partner is not in individual therapy), one partner is put in the position to regulate their partner's parts.

Regulating these parts every now and then through healthy coregulation is not problematic, but the dynamic that can occur by constantly relying on that regulation can get complicated. If one partner's childlike parts get attached to the other's adult parts, there can be dynamic shifts that mimic parentification (when parents rely on their children for support rather than providing it) or hierarchical power dynamics. I have seen this be problematic in areas of intimacy, especially with survivors of childhood sexual abuse. If one partner is responsible for regulating the younger parts of the other, then, when everyone is back "online" after the situation has calmed and both want to engage in sexual activity, there are still young parts of one partner that are now complexly attached to the other. This can lead to things becoming very complicated very quickly. (We will discuss this more in the chapters related to sex and boundaries.)

Rejection

Another possible response to a partner's distress might be rejection, the causes of which range from discomfort with vulnerability and "big feelings" to frustration over the inability to "fix" the situation, or even shame (e.g., if the cause of your partner's distress can be interpreted as your "fault"). Rejection feeds into the "dance of parts" and, like rescuing, will likely cause more stress and frustration. This is because it can also be a major trigger for partners who have a history of being rejected, so different attachment styles and parts become involved and the protectors of each partner emerge and engage with each other.

Reassurance

Providing gentle reassurance is an ideal relational option that allows everyone in the relationship to validate each other's emotions without being responsible for "fixing" them, and without invalidating or running from vulnerability. This can sound like, "You're really upset right now. Your feelings are absolutely valid, and I hear you. What do you need to reassure yourself that you're safe?" Such reassurance enables the partners in a relationship to maintain distance from each other (by putting the responsibility for self-soothing back on themselves) while still feeling heard and validated in their experiences. Providing reassurance versus rescuing or rejecting can be difficult at first, especially if there are already dynamics in place that are relying on rescuing or rejecting for regulation. Practicing this frequently while also reassuring your partner that you are *not* abandoning them will be essential.

I often see individuals feel very rejected and/or abandoned when their partner(s) take a step back from rescuing and attempt to reassure instead. If you experience this, reminding your partner that you still love them and that you are not going anywhere and prompting them gently to find their Self energy is a good start. You want your partner(s) to start developing an attachment to their adult self so they can regulate their own hard emotions versus consistently relying on you to provide that rescue. Of course you will always try to be there for the relational connection and emotional support that comes with being in a relationship with someone, but that is different from constant internal emotional regulation of your partner. Remember, it takes time!

Bonding Through Trauma—When Two or More Partners Have a Trauma History

When more than one individual in a relationship has a trauma history, that shared history brings with it a special bond, a brotherhood in arms, a shared knowing. Because of this implicit understanding, it is common for individuals who have a trauma history to be drawn to one another. This is a type of *bonding through trauma*, which is different from trauma bonding, where there is a totalitarian power dynamic when the captive falls in love with the captor (a.k.a. Stockholm syndrome).[28] Bonding through trauma is a **connection of activation**, meaning where parts recognize parts, dysregulation is known, and mutual dysregulation can be focused on a mutual enemy: the perpetrators of the past.

I often see this connection of activation present at the beginning of a relationship, when there is mutual outrage at past experiences and blanket understanding when triggers happen. This initial understanding is very different from what someone may experience in relationships where one partner does not have a history of trauma and therefore cannot viscerally understand the experience. Because

---

[28] Jeeva Kanesarajah et al., "Unit Cohesion, Traumatic Exposure and Mental Health of Military Personnel," *Occupational Medicine* 66, no. 4 (2016): 308–315, https://doi.org/10.1093/occmed/kqw009.

of this understanding and validation, however, relationships bonded through trauma can intensify and escalate quickly. That feeling of shared emotional drama can feel like significant emotional intimacy, but it is a dynamic of side-by-side alliance braced to fight outwardly instead of a face-to-face, deeply internal connection. While emotional drama and intensity can be very exciting and temporarily stimulating, it is not the same as true and lasting emotional intimacy.

Queer Application—Double Bonding Through Trauma

Any identity for which you fear retribution and harm due to the expression of that identity is traumatic. Therefore, being queer in today's society is traumatic. As opposed to other dimensions of diversity, sexual identity is not something around which queer individuals can typically rally their family of origin to find support in sameness or shared identity; in fact, individuals who identify as queer are often rejected by their families of origin.

Queer relationships already involve a heightened likelihood of establishing bonding through trauma because the trauma *is* the queer identity itself in a heteronormative world. Therefore, individuals who identify as queer tend to turn inward for emotional nurturing, sticking within our pods and specifically sticking within our relationships. It can be difficult, at times, to seek social support outside of our queer pods and the queer community, which limits our options for emotional support, our exposure to alternative sources of safety and affirmation, and the alternative perspectives needed to avoid dependence on our partners for complete emotional support. This makes romantic relationships, especially those in which one or more individuals have a trauma history, even more complicated.

I see a lot of codependence in queer relationships because of this, and it tends to be a product of necessity and survival. Add into the mix a history of interpersonal trauma by one or more of the members of a partnership, and an expounded recipe for increased codependence, enmeshment (becoming emotionally dependent and entangled with your partner), and part responses results. Members of these relationships often have difficulty separating three types of bonding: bonding through trauma related to queer identity, bonding through trauma related to interpersonal traumatic experiences, and bonding through the levels of intimacy, communication, and connection found in any standard relationship without trauma.

Queer couples have to work to deepen their bonds far beyond their mutual enemy of a traumatizing world and toward authentic intimacy. In relationship counseling, this might mean identifying areas that strengthen the attachment between partners and focusing on boundaries, internal patterns of communication, internalization of traumatic experiences, and safety, rather than rallying together against outward issues. Relationships cannot survive exclusively on vacations and common enemies, so truly digging deep and consciously putting effort into knowing ourselves and introducing our true selves to our partners is essential.

Digging Deeper Activity

How might you reassure your partner that you are not rejecting them outright but are encouraging them to find internal resources in a loving and supportive way? How might you sit with the discomfort that might arise when you don't rescue them?

Digging Even Deeper...

What are some ways that might allow you to show up more authentically in your current relationships? How might you deepen your bonds beyond the double-bonding through trauma and toward authentic intimacy?

_____

_____

_____

_____

_____

_____

_____

_____

Chapter 6
Dances of Partners aka Dances of Parts

I'm like a tree. My leaves might change color,
but my roots are the same.
— Rose Namajunas

In a relationship, we have an innate desire to swoop in and help out our partners when they are in distress. We might want to hold them, nurture them, comfort them, and take away all their pain, frustration, and sadness, especially if they have a trauma history and we know how difficult life has been for them. The key is to provide healthy **coregulation** to the partner, meaning we use our own regulated emotions and calm states to instill calm and regulation in our partners, and our partners use our regulation and calm to relax enough to find internal resources to regulate themselves. To do this, we must first find our own levels of self-compassion and awareness and recognize our own needs for regulation, "unblending" (recognizing when a part is responding versus our adult self), and enmeshment.

We want our partners to find stability in us and then use their own internal regulation processes to get themselves back online. Throwing them a life preserver when they are drowning is great, but we want to give them enough love, reassurance, and steadiness to help them catch their breath and then swim to shore under their own power. Ideally, their "own power" is the key, and this can be tricky. Often, partners with a history of trauma have an exceedingly difficult time regulating themselves because their many parts are trying to protect them from pain. So, when an activating event like a fight or perceived rejection triggers a partner, their system becomes dysregulated and a part takes over to protect them from feeling those big pains. Something in their system runs around panicking—wide-eyed and flailing its hands in the air—which presents outwardly as yelling, pulling away, desperately trying to connect, feeling intense drives to use and abuse substances, dissociating, and frantically needing reassurance. When this happens, it is our partner's dysregulation. In these instances, if we can recognize what is happening and are "online" with our adult self, we can *attune* to our partners in a healthy way. Attunement simply means paying attention to our partners' emotions,[29] and really leaning into their experience. Through attunement, we can notice the distress in our partners, validate their experiences, and provide an empathetic coregulation and connection with them that helps them feel heard and seen.

Coregulation vs. Codependence

Being cued into our partners' needs, triggers, and moods can be healthy and helpful, but only when there are established boundaries.

---

[29] Una McCluskey, Derek Roger, and Poppy Nash, "A Preliminary Study of the Role of Attunement in Adult Psychotherapy," *Human Relations* 50, no. 10 (2016): 1261–1273, https://doi.org/10.1177/001872679705001004

Without boundaries, we may find ourselves being pulled into the emotional distress of our partners or feeling that we cannot have an emotional experience outside of our partners' distress, which are indicators of **codependence**. This can occur in a variety of ways, typically when our partners' parts are driving the bus instead of their adult selves. When we are activated or dysregulated at the same time as our partners, when our upset fuels theirs, when we cannot have a good day unless they are having a good day, and when our partners are dependent on us for regulation, these are signs of codependency. Whereas coregulation is using our calm adult state to calm our partner's dysregulation with *healthy boundaries*, codependency occurs when either dysregulation begets dysregulation or when parts become *dependent* on the regulation of our partners—either where life preservers are expected or where everyone is drowning.

A common dynamic that I see among the partners I work with is this 'part connected to adult self' regulation becoming expected in a codependent relationship. For example, if Jane gets triggered frequently and becomes dysregulated often but she has not cultivated the ability to manage her own distress, she might become reliant on Rachel to talk her down, coach her through breathing, and challenge her negative, self-harming thoughts. If that younger child part of Jane that feels out of control begins to see Rachel as a primary attachment figure, it can cause some problematic relational fallout. Some of Jane's parts could see Rachel as a mothering figure, which could impact the intimacy, sex, and adult connection in the relationship long term. It could also trigger any parts that may have a history of differential power dynamics due to abusive situations. So, while Rachel might try to help via immediacy, she may inadvertently cause more relationship difficulty down the road because these parts don't have the same breadth of awareness, connection, or timeframe as her or Jane's adult self. In addition, consistently providing regulation to

Jane does not allow her to practice regulating herself, which further entrenches her dependance on Rachel.

Setting boundaries with our partners related to coregulation can help us maintain our focus and efforts on our own internal work. In turn, this allows us to repair attachment ruptures in both our partners' and our own parts and begin to securely attach us to our adult selves.

Another way we can see this mismatch is through **codependent attunement**, which is a little deeper of a dive than codependence. We can start to hyperattune to our partners to try to *proactively* prevent their distress by keeping them from getting too upset, too sad, too angry, or too triggered. This can lead to us trying to predict the emotions and actions of our partners, creating dialogues in which we tell ourselves stories and fill in the blanks with our own assumptions of what our partners need.

At times, our partners may not even know what they need, so trying to predict it can cause more frustration and dysregulation. Predicting their needs does not allow our partners to develop an inner awareness of their own internal resources of curiosity and problem solving, so they are often left wondering what they are feeling, what they need, and how they can meet those needs. Their window of tolerance does not have the opportunity to grow independently, so we are put in the role of being responsible for helping them recognize safety (referred to in the field as "neuroception-by-proxy") by proactively fawning, providing regulation after their shame or anger response, or rescuing them from distress. Figure 8 illustrates codependent attunement in action.

In this example, Partner B is dysregulated, so Partner A either steps into a parts-based manager/mitigator role or is required to be

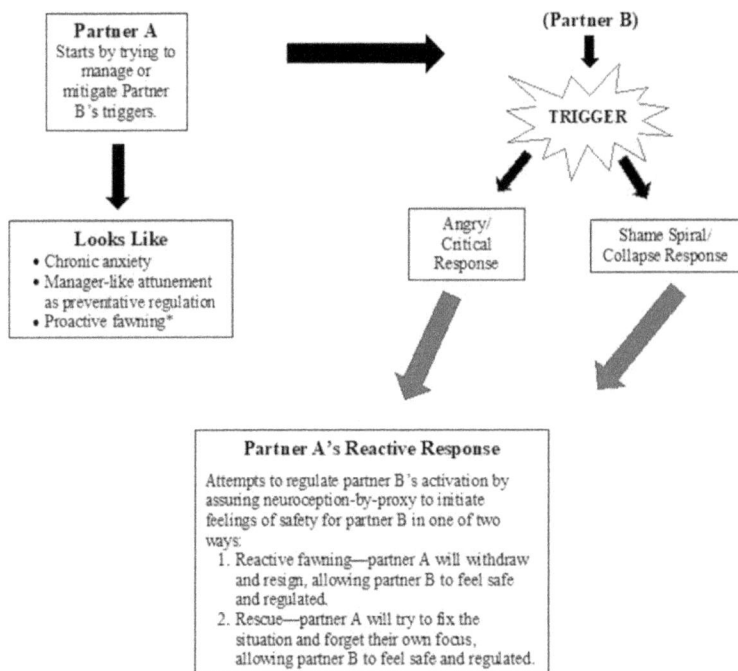

Partner A
Starts by trying to manage or mitigate Partner B's triggers.

(Partner B)

TRIGGER

Looks Like
- Chronic anxiety
- Manager-like attunement as preventative regulation
- Proactive fawning*

Angry/ Critical Response

Shame Spiral/ Collapse Response

Partner A's Reactive Response

Attempts to regulate partner B's activation by assuring neuroception-by-proxy to initiate feelings of safety for partner B in one of two ways:
1. Reactive fawning—partner A will withdraw and resign, allowing partner B to feel safe and regulated.
2. Rescue—partner A will try to fix the situation and forget their own focus, allowing partner B to feel safe and regulated.

*Proactive fawning example: "I don't want to express discomfort or emotion because I don't want to be a burden. If I bring the energy down, I might cause my partner to retreat, panic, stress more, or have their own reaction. Then I'd have to take care of my partner by abandoning my issues and not getting my needs met. Instead, I'll give in or remove all barriers to mitigate my partner's hard emotions or stressors so they don't have to feel discomfort. While this means that I won't be able to freely express my anger, sadness, or relational conflict, it also means that I won't have to take care of my partner's related reactions. And that seems like less emotional labor than the fallout from being honest, open, and vulnerable."

Figure 8. Diagram of Codependent Attunement.

in an adult state. This mitigation or responsive codependence does not encourage either partner to look inside and learn more about themselves or their needs, nor does it leave room for the partners to speak their truths.

Neurobiological Fact

Coregulation can only happen if someone can safely access their vagus nerve through calmly connecting to their adult self. Vagus nerve inhibition happens when survival mode sets in and reduces access to the frontal lobes of the brain, which are responsible for empathy, perspective, and a sense of "a bigger picture." When activated, the vagus nerve moves a person into either a sympathetic nervous system response where tension, anger, and judgment live, or a dorsal vagal response where shame, withdrawal, and disconnection live.[30] Identifying your autonomic awareness can assist in recognizing when relationships don't feel reciprocal and allows you to identify when your parts become active or increase their activity due to protective factors or protectors of the "exiles," a.k.a. "big, hard feelings."

The Dance of Over and Underperforming

Healthy relationships have high levels of reciprocity in which the give and take equals itself out in the end. This give and take can be seen in a variety of ways, either in day-to-day tasks like "You go to work, and I'll take care of the kiddos" or as emotional balances like "I'm having a tough day. Will you take the dog for a walk tonight so I can just chill on the couch?" The stressors of life commonly require one partner to "take the reins" and assist in supporting or regulating the other partner through a crisis or difficult transition. However, if this lack of balance becomes the new norm for your relationship

---

[30] Stephen W. Porges, "Polyvagal Theory: A Science of Safety," *Frontiers in Integrative Neuroscience* 16, no. 871227 (2022): 1–15, https://doi.org/10.3389/fnint.2022.871227.

dynamic, resulting in one partner's needs becoming prioritized more frequently than another's, it can feel draining, frustrating, and unsafe. Safety is a cornerstone of any level of vulnerability, but it is especially important for relationships in which one or both individuals have a history of trauma.

Because our brains and bodies are constantly scanning the environment for threats to our safety, there is a very real possibility that they will find threats in everyday life. When it comes to relational safety, we might have parts that say, "They aren't physically harmful, yelling, or abusive in a way that is a threat to my safety and might warrant raising the red flags." However, power differentials and displacement in power dynamics can be threatening to a system as well.[31] This can especially be seen in partners who have an individual history of their needs being seen as not important or were raised in situations where their emotions and sense of safety were not prioritized. When these individuals are put in a caretaking role for the purpose of continually regulating their partner, they can feel ignored or that their needs are being minimized because it is reminiscent of their past. As any threat can, this can activate their nervous system and make vulnerability difficult. If a partner does not feel that it is safe to be vulnerable, it can lead to a lack of attunement, thus impacting bigger themes, such as attachment and sex. That lack of attunement will likely present a myriad of part responses:

- Proactive Parts
  - Manager-esque criticizing: "If you do things this way, they'll be easier and you won't be so upset."

---

[31] Sue Johnson and Brent Bradley, "Emotionally Focused Couple Therapy: Creating Loving Relationships," in *The Wiley-Blackwell Handbook of Family Psychology*, eds. James H. Bray and Mark Stanton (Oxford: Blackwell Publishing, 2009), 402–415, https://doi.org/10.1002/9781444310238.ch27.

- Proactive fawning: "Whatever you need, I'll give you before you even ask, even if it means giving up what I need."
- Proactive distancing or withdrawing: "I don't trust that I can be vulnerable, so I'm not going to put myself out there."
- Reactive Parts
  - Anger flares: "It's not fair that I have to be in control all the time! I want to be able to fall apart too!"
  - Reactive fawning: "I'll do whatever I have to do for things to be fixed so that you'll stop being upset. It feels scary and unsteady when you're upset!"
  - Rescuing: "You'll be okay. I'm here. I'll take away all the hard stuff for you. I'll be stable and steady for us both."
  - Blaming: "You should be able to take care of these things yourself!"
  - Reactive withdrawing: "I'm hurt because I want this to feel equal."

This dance of over and underperforming can continue building momentum until it becomes a difficult habit to break or reverse. At times, the supported partner will have parts that feel resentful if the homeostasis changes because they have become accustomed to and reliant on their partner doing the regulation work for them. There may be scared parts that feel abandoned, angry parts that lash out, and parts that feel like the relationship is shaky. In these cases, we can provide reassurance that we are not abandoning them, mad at them, or rejecting them in any way, but are trying to recognize patterns that impact our ability to feel vulnerable and heard. We can enlist our partners' help to assist us in discovering relationship reciprocity. The logistical balance is different for every relationship, but reciprocity is nonnegotiable. Figure 9 illustrates the cycle of over and underperforming.

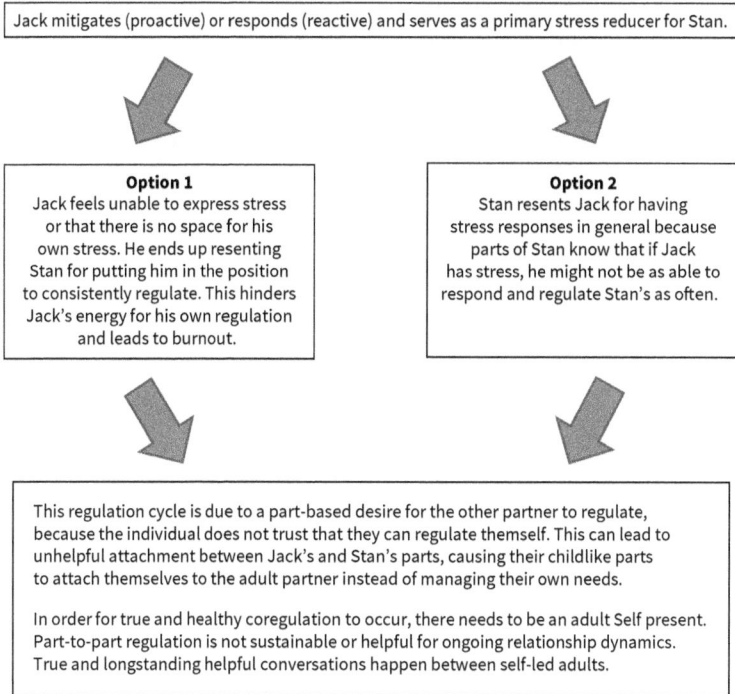

Jack mitigates (proactive) or responds (reactive) and serves as a primary stress reducer for Stan.

Option 1
Jack feels unable to express stress or that there is no space for his own stress. He ends up resenting Stan for putting him in the position to consistently regulate. This hinders Jack's energy for his own regulation and leads to burnout.

Option 2
Stan resents Jack for having stress responses in general because parts of Stan know that if Jack has stress, he might not be as able to respond and regulate Stan's as often.

This regulation cycle is due to a part-based desire for the other partner to regulate, because the individual does not trust that they can regulate themself. This can lead to unhelpful attachment between Jack's and Stan's parts, causing their childlike parts to attach themselves to the adult partner instead of managing their own needs.

In order for true and healthy coregulation to occur, there needs to be an adult Self present. Part-to-part regulation is not sustainable or helpful for ongoing relationship dynamics. True and longstanding helpful conversations happen between self-led adults.

Figure 9. The Cycle of Over- and Underperforming.

Figure 10 demonstrates the different part attachments between Allison and Jessica, who are trying to work out a new relationship dynamic.

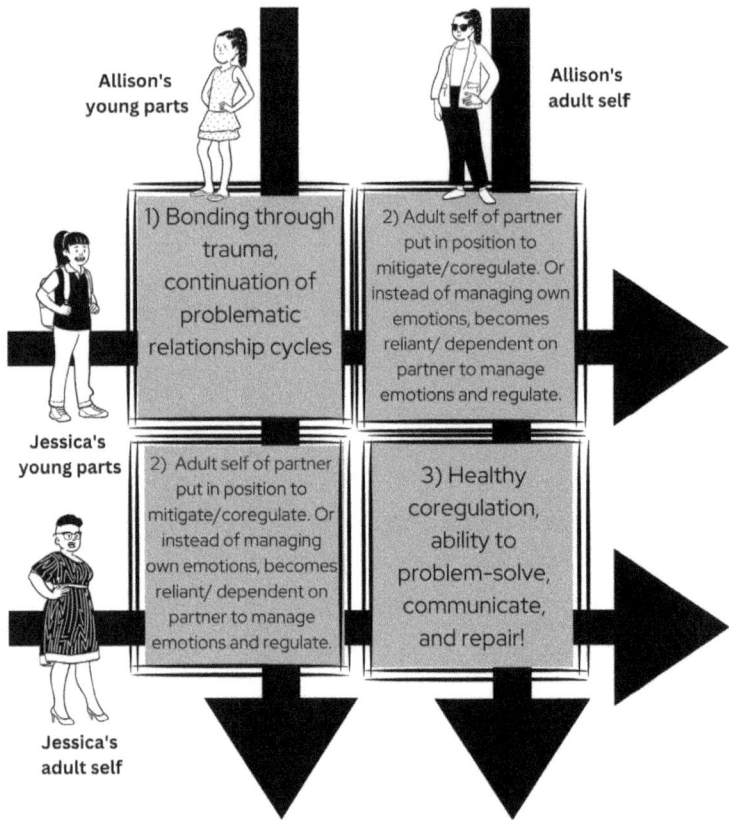

Figure 10. Common Relationship Dynamics.

The figure contains the following labels and boxes:

Allison's young parts

Allison's adult self

Jessica's young parts

Jessica's adult self

1) Bonding through trauma, continuation of problematic relationship cycles

2) Adult self of partner put in position to mitigate/coregulate. Or instead of managing own emotions, becomes reliant/ dependent on partner to manage emotions and regulate.

2) Adult self of partner put in position to mitigate/coregulate. Or instead of managing own emotions, becomes reliant/ dependent on partner to manage emotions and regulate.

3) Healthy coregulation, ability to problem-solve, communicate, and repair!

1. When Jessica's and Allison's parts attach to one another, it can lead to bonding through trauma, codependence, and continuation of problematic cycles.
2. If Allison frequently rescues and mitigates Jessica's emotional reactivity, a different dynamic of codependent attunement will develop.
3. In the final option, both women's adult selves are connecting, creating healthy coregulation, opportunity for the eight Cs, and communication that is productive and constructive.

Attachment Injuries in the Dance of Parts

An **attachment injury** is a betrayal of trust and abandonment at a crucial moment of need.[32] This is completely unique to the person or partner and is focused on the attachment significance, not its content. For example, one partner may cheat on another, but in that couple's culture, this is not uncommon and thus to them is not a major injury to their attachment. In another relationship, infidelity might be a deal breaker.

Attachment injuries are a form of relationship trauma that can define the relationship as insecure. It can be a singular event or an insidious breaking of a relationship "bone." This bone will not heal properly without injury intervention (usually relationship therapy) and will continue to appear over and over in fights that include a common thread of an attachment wound. In queer folx, attachment injuries present in typical heteronormative ways, but there can also be added dynamics, such as rejection of yourself or a partner, that are based on self-loathing, internalized homophobia, or fear. This can echo past events of rejection by family, friends, and society, and sharing them can be very impactful in the comfort and confidence of a current relationship that includes trust, safety, and stability and allows all partners to know they are cared for and loved.

---

[32] Rebecca E. Halchuk, Judy A. Makinen, and Susan M. Johnson, "Resolving Attachment Injuries in Couples Using Emotionally Focused Therapy: A Three-Year Follow-Up," *Journal of Couple & Relationship Therapy* 9, no. 1 (2010): 31–47, https://doi.org/10.1080/15332690903473069.

Example:

James comes to counseling with his partner Felix. James reports that Felix pulls away in public, sometimes introducing James as his "friend," and after sex, becomes cold and emotionally closed off. When James tries to talk to Felix about it, Felix gets angry and walks away. When they are alone at home or around their mutual friends, Felix is very attentive and holds James's hand or even kisses him. James reports not knowing what to expect and that Felix's actions make him unsure about the relationship, question how much Felix actually cares, and even makes him feel ashamed of public displays of affection at times. Felix tries to reassure James that he loves him, but James is starting to feel like he cannot trust Felix to stand up for him or their relationship if things were to get difficult. James reports, "I can't ever tell when he wants me to hop back in the closet, and it's really messing with how hard I worked to be proud of who I am."

Digging Deeper Activity

Think back to a time when you may have overperformed or underperformed in a relationship. What did that look like and feel like? Did it become a pattern? Do a check-in with your parts ... how did it feel to be in that role? What is it like in your current relationship? Are there times when you feel things are unequal in a way that is written into your dynamic? What might you do to change that and perhaps encourage reassurance versus rescuing (if you feel you are overperforming)? What other dances can you identify? What push/pull patterns do you see?

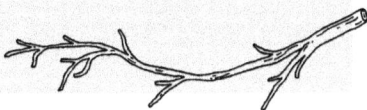

_____

_____

_____

_____

_____

_____

_____

_____

_____

Part 3

The "Now What" of the "Relationship Stuff"

Chapter 7
Repair Work

The roots of a tree control the tree and the roots
of a thought control the thinking.
The "roots" of your thoughts control your reactions.
– Master Soon

In any relationship, we are going to fight with our partners. It *will* happen. What matters is how we manage it and grow from it. In relationships, we all make mistakes, and that's okay! Mistakes are how we learn together, get closer to one another, and better care for each other. When we resolve one argument, that does not mean another will never happen. But when it does, we can be better prepared to handle it. Trauma is something that never fully "goes away," but the more we take it head-on and address our needs with ourselves and loved ones in healthy and communicative ways, the easier it becomes to manage.

There are going to be times when you screw up. I still screw up—royally! But you are here. You are asking the right questions and learning lots of new information. You are showing up. This is vital!

By being here, you are demonstrating that you have faith in your relationship. You have a genuine desire to try to figure out how to make it work. Now, let's give that momentum some direction and see how you can use it when shit still feels so hard.

Over the last several chapters, we reviewed many of the things that go on internally within us, things that go on internally within our partners, and the dances that we experience within our relationships. Now we are going to turn toward what to do when things go awry, as we know they will. I don't say this is a means of doom and gloom; I say this as a way of embracing the reality that is the human condition. We are not meant to be perfect creatures. We are meant to learn, grow, and adapt as new knowledge and stimuli come into our consciousness. So, as we learn new things about our relationships and the way we interact with one another and our environment, those things will shift and change as well. Knowing why our partners react a certain way allows us to find ways to diffuse a situation. Knowing why we respond or interpret situations in certain ways allows us to take a pause before we respond, be deeply curious as to why our partner gets so hurt when we neglect to acknowledge a special day, and understand why it feels like the air gets sucked out of our lungs when our partners don't feel like being touched at a certain moment. This curiosity and learning, this adaptation to new information, helps our relationship grow.

Now we shift our attention to the ways we can catch ourselves in the midst of a fight or argument. We will learn how to step back and come together in healing and healthy ways to navigate through hard conversations, common stressors, and everyday nuances. I refer to the work that we will be doing together as **repair work**. Repair work is, in its most basic sense, repairing old wounds from childhood and/or past traumatic relationships and/or the wounds that happen in new relationships (and are likely caused by the old stuff, as we just explored). Repair work can happen individually, as well as between us and our partners.[33]

Let's dive deeper into this framework by looking at the tools we need, using an acronym I created through observation of common relationship dances and struggles: "PEACE TALKS." Each letter of the acronym stands for an element of a conversation or interaction that helps us navigate a potentially trigger-filled minefield:

P—Pause	T—Take Ownership
E—Emotion	A—Attune Outwardly
A—Attune Inwardly	L—Listen
C—Compassion	K—Keep a Cool Head
E—Express	S—See Each Other Anew

Repair Work Through "PEACE TALKS"

Say your partner texts to ask you whether you care if they go out for drinks with a friend after work. Since you already had plans with them for a quiet night at home, your initial reaction bubbles up quickly! You lash out at them, firing off a text that tells them they obviously don't care about you. You start spiraling internally about the status of the relationship and how much they must actually not care. You start feeling really down and depressed and recognize a panic attack coming on. You have jumped from zero to 60 in less than a minute. Now it is time for some "PEACE TALKS" skills. The "PEACE" portion takes place internally and individually, and the "TALKS" section focuses on coming back together and repairing relational dynamics.

---

[33] John M. Gottman and Nan Silver, *7 Principles for Making Marriage Work: A Practical Guide from the Country's Foremost Relationship Expert* (New York: Harmony Books, 2015), 26–27.

P: Pause

Take a time out if you need to spatially and/or emotionally take a break. This might mean stopping texting, leaving the room, or asking for space, for example. Pausing to take a break does not mean separating to manipulate or escape a hard conversation; instead, it means taking space to reorient, become grounded, take some deep breaths, and gain some clarity. This can be a difficult thing to do when you are feeling very anxious and need to be reassured or heard. At these times, it is incredibly important to recognize that drive within yourself so that you can resolve the situation completely in the moment. Remember, once you are activated to this extent, no real repair can happen. A part of you has taken over and is charged with such emotion that you cannot actually hear or respond in a healthy or helpful way. So, taking a moment to breathe and gain some proximal and emotional distance for the purpose of centering yourself is an essential first step in any relationship repair work.

This may take some time! If you feel yourself trying to reengage with an agenda to be heard or prove a point—you need to stay in this space a little longer. It isn't until you can feel the charge dissipate and the energy shift, that you can move on to the next step.

E: Emotion

Once you have gained some space with a pause, the next step is to listen internally and get curious about any emotions you are feeling. The first thing you will likely feel is being PISSED: *I'm angry! I'm disappointed. I'm sad. I'm scared.* As you listen internally and become curious, you may begin to notice that even though your initial emotion is anger, there are a few other emotions deeper down that carry a little bit more weight. These feelings are usually at the center of why you are reacting the way you are. They are the mobilized parts of you that are protecting you from feeling strong, scary, and/or sad emotions. Anger is just a shield. When you pull back the top layer and get really curious about what is going on underneath the anger, you can start asking bigger questions about what you feel and why.

A: Attune Inwardly

After identifying the emotions you are feeling, attune to what is actually going on underneath those immediate emotions and reactions. Ask yourself questions like, *Why am I feeling this way? What are some of my unmet attachment needs? Is this my anxious attachment that is afraid of being abandoned, or is this my avoidant attachment that wants to push away vulnerability? Did I trust too hard?* Lean in and really listen to what is going on inside, and then validate that experience. Continue using those attunement skills on yourself. Hear yourself. What are those little parts scared of?

C: Compassion

Needing comfort while also fearing vulnerability and abandonment is okay. It is understandable because of your past. Now that you have recognized where those big feelings are coming from, though, extend some compassion to yourself. It is okay to be scared. Look at what you have been through and how far you have come. Your past is a part of you, and all parts of you are welcome. All emotions you feel are valid. Recognize that you got mad because you were hurt. Because of your history, you felt like you were not important, and that made you feel unsafe and scared of abandonment. You lashed out. Getting mad is understandable; this shit is hard! Just remember that even though it is okay and valid to be scared, and it is understandable *why* the fear mobilized into anger, lashing out at your partner is *not* okay.

E: Express

After sitting with your emotions for a minute and doing some deep inner work to figure out what happened and why, you can better express your *real* emotions, needs, and fears to your partner. Ask yourself what you might want your partner to know about how you are feeling and how you could feel reassured. Then see whether they are ready to reengage in a conversation. If they are not, they might still be working through their own PEACE steps and may need a bit more time. Take that opportunity to continue doing inner work. Reassure yourself that their need for more space is important so that you can come back together from a place of calm, compassionate, and productive energy. Reentering charged conversations too soon can cause destructive and painful retriggering that needs to be repaired from even bigger rifts.

T: Take Ownership

Once you recognize that the way you *felt* was valid but your *actions* might have been hurtful, take ownership of that and start working outwardly. Emotions are valid, and actions have consequences. Claim your own reactions and responses, even if they were big and hurtful. Identify, don't justify! Apologize if needed (and it probably is), but apologize for the action, not the underlying emotion: "I'm sorry I yelled at you." "I apologize for calling you names." "I never meant to hurt your feelings." These are all true statements that don't negate your underlying emotion or excuse your behavior. Your intent and impact may very well be maligned. Recognize both!

It is essential that you stay with your apology and not justify your actions. Statements such as "I'm sorry I was loud, but you really piss me off!" or "I wouldn't have gotten so mad if you had just listened and not been so critical!" take ownership away from you and place blame on the other person for "making" you do something. This is called a "yes, but" or "zap caboose" approach, which is literally the deflating of all apology energy. It will not have the desired effect, so you will likely become even more angry and restart the fight: "I'm sorry I hung up on you (yes!)... but you really made me mad, and you know I can't stand it when you say I'm acting like my father." ZAP! This just took all the positive momentum from the apology and zapped it away. If you are starting to rehash old wounds, STOP! Refer back to "P: Pause" and take some space.

Now imagine truly owning that you hurt their feelings: "I'm sorry I said those things... (Pause)... I never, ever mean to make you feel unseen." ... pause ... How lovely and refreshing would that feel—for both of you?! Imagine receiving this from your partner (let the simple joy of that wash over you)—and when you get down to it, we all want to be genuinely validated and seen. This is a good first step.

Practice taking ownership. This step is a doozy, and your loud protector parts will want to be vocal about their grievances. They have a time and place, but the ownership and apology step is *not* it. Practice some internal reassurance and refocus on the task at hand.

A: Attune Outwardly

Once you are each able to own your individual actions, typically your guards will begin to lower a bit. You will be able to see that there is more behind the loud words and slammed doors. But, in order to really engage, you need to pay attention to your partner. Turn to them and really listen with your ears, your body language, and your emotions. Lean in and acknowledge their pain. What is their body saying? Did their shoulders drop and their posture relax? Did their volume lower? Are those tears in their eyes? Really listen to one another with your whole selves. When they say that they are scared, do you see the pain? Can you feel your own response to their pain?

L: Listen

Now knowing what your partner is feeling, listen to what they might need from you to feel safer, less triggered, or more attached in a healthy way. At this stage, you are ready to listen to each other's expression of needs (which you discovered in the PEACE stages). You are expressing to each other what the underlying attachment need is. What are you scared of? How did that show up when you were trying to talk earlier and started fighting? What led to what? Walk each other through what you both learned when you were curious with yourselves.

K: Keep a Cool Head

Staying in a place of attunement to better attach is a tough one. Many times throughout PEACE TALKS, you might catch yourself getting defensive, paying too much attention to the "What about me?!" parts. Keep a cool head, because you will get a chance to have your partner listen to you in this way too! Remember, this is not a competition and there is no "winner." If you find yourself too caught up in trying to be "right," take a pause. Trying to be "right" is a sign that your adult self might not be as online as you would like and a protector part is trying to grab the microphone. That protector might be feeling that you are giving in too much and are therefore at risk of getting hurt. Name that! Talk to your partner about it: "I'm starting to get defensive and might need some reassurance that we'll get to talk about [xyz]." This might require a time out or break. That's okay! Breaks are not failures. In fact, they are excellent examples that you are both learning when you are activated and when you need time to breathe before doing or saying something relationally destructive. This is progress!

S: See Each Other Anew

After stripping away the protector reactions to better understand what is going on underneath the surface, you can better communicate, attune, validate, and meet each other's needs. Take this time of vulnerability to come up with some ways you can reassure, provide comfort, and be a safe place for each other. What might it look like when you have another triggering moment like this? What might help provide reassurance to your partner that you love them and they are important, even if you are still going to dinner with a friend? What can your partner do to make sure you feel safe and heard when you are feeling scared or frustrated? This is a time to make requests as to how you can each speak directly to those underlying attachment needs and calm the storm before it happens—or at least deescalate the situation so it does not reach hurricane status.

How This Plays Out in a Real Fight

After a really nasty fight during which Steve said things that hurt Bob's feelings, they each took some time to breathe and separate from the agitated energy. Once they were ready to come back together, they sat down and started to discuss the fight.

Bob: Steven, you really hurt me. You said some awful things! (*Identifies the injury*)

Steve: I know. I just lost it. I don't even remember half of what I said, but I know it wasn't good. I know that I hurt you, and I'm truly sorry. (*Acknowledges and apologizes genuinely without justifying behavior*)

Bob: Thank you for saying that. It really scared me. I didn't think you were capable of getting so angry! It reminded me of when my dad used to yell at me and hit me. (*Allowed to express deeper feelings and connections*)

Steve: I know that he was not a nice man. That must have been really terrifying. Please know that that isn't me. I can get mad sometimes, but I would never hurt you like that. (*Continues to acknowledge feelings, validate without question, and stay in the moment with Bob without diving into a shame spiral*)

Bob: He was capable of such terrible things. He made me feel so small. I never thought I was going to survive my childhood. I promised myself I wouldn't even have to feel that way again. It was so scary to feel so small back then! (*Prompted to go deeper into feelings and deep attachment wounds, fears, and foundational ruptures*)

Steve: I hear you—I do. (*Reaches for Bob to provide physical comfort and holds him while he cries*) I am not him. I will always protect you and love you, even if I get mad. That anger is my issue.

It's not a reflection of who you are or your worth. (*Needs to hear it, feel it, not get defensive, and acknowledge the depth of pain without diving into shame*)

Bob: (*Leans into the hug and cries harder. He feels heard, loved, and coregulated and starts to rebuild trust*)

Let's externalize this using an example presented during an Emotionally Focused Couples Therapy training I attended in 2022:[34] You are not paying attention and run over a dog. Being an animal lover, you pull over and race to the dog to take it to the vet. When you approach the dog, rather than licking and loving on you, it bites, wriggles, and tries to run away, despite your efforts to try to help and heal the situation. You need to be calm, understanding, loving, and caring for the dog, consistently reassuring it and providing constant understanding that it is scared, hurt, and does not know what is going to happen. In this analogy, the dog represents your partner. You may not have been paying attention or a protector was driving the car, so an accident occurred. Of course you love your partner and would not intentionally hurt them. After an "accident," you might try to repair the situation immediately, but your partner might be hurt and will likely not want to snuggle up and get cozy with you. Instead, they might lash out at you or push you away. Be patient, own your actions, and provide consistent reassurance in order to rebuild trust and confidence in the safety of the relationship.

---

[34] Emotionally Focused Therapy – Externship, presented by ICEEFT Trainer Kathryn de Bruin, September 23–24, 2022 and September 31-October 1, 2022, Austin, Texas, http://joexcantueft.com/externships/

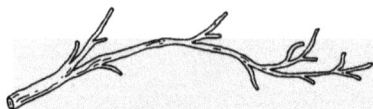

Digging Deeper: Practice Your Apology

Let's practice what you just learned and try to apologize in a way that does not immediately zap away the emotion or message behind it.

Think of a recent fight you had with your partner during which you said something pretty awful (don't worry, I've done it too!). Internally recognize and validate your reasons for lashing out. Maybe they said hurtful things too. Maybe a part of you was trying to push them away because things felt too intense. Maybe someone else was driving the bus. Those things are all valid and real, and changing your behavior is really hard. But keep trying!

Recognize that your adult self did not mean to hurt your partner, because your adult self is compassionate and calm. Regardless of _why_ you said what you said, though, you still might have hurt them. Imagine taking ownership of that action and asking your partner what they might need to feel safe with you. Imagine apologizing for your action, without including a justification or explanation. This might look like, "Babe, I yelled at you when we were fighting, and I said some really hurtful things. I'm really sorry."

What might your apology look like?

_____

_____

_____

_____

_____

_____

_____

_____

_____

_____

_____

_____

_____

_____

_____

_____

_____

_____

Chapter 8

Boundaries: What They Are and How They Look in Trauma Survivors

*Don't set [your trees] on fire trying
to keep others warm.*
– Penny Reid (adapted)

Boundaries. We talked about these several times throughout the previous chapters, but what are they really? Boundaries are personal. They delineate the lines of expectation, comfort, and safety. They can help us define what we are comfortable with related to our bodies, emotions, and time preferences. Boundaries help us maintain safety and keep us from becoming depleted in a variety of ways. Some people think of boundaries as hard and fast lines, or rules. Others think of them as guidelines. How you define boundaries is completely up to you. The beautiful thing is that *you* get to choose what feels good, right, and safe for *you*.

Why Boundaries Are So Important

Boundaries keep us from becoming too enmeshed with others, prevent us from giving all of ourselves away, and are a first step in listening to and respecting those voices inside of us that let us know when things feel scary. With boundaries, we can set a standard, an expectation. And boundaries are needed in all of our relationships, whether its coworkers invading our flow, friends calling us any time of the day or night, or family showing up to our home unannounced. Setting a boundary can be seen as revoking a privilege that a person was never supposed to have in the first place. We also need boundaries when relationships or lovers want more of us than we are comfortable giving, when children invade the bathroom regardless of the closed door, or when your boss asks you to stay late for the third night in a row.

One primary thing to remember about boundaries is that they are personally established to determine what *you* will and will not accept. They are not delineations of what others can do and cannot be used to dictate other's actions or emotions. This can be tricky. Instead of: "You can't do that," it needs to be, "I won't tolerate that." This is an important distinction, because the latter leaves less room for individuals to argue with the boundary since it is based on your behaviors, needs, and what you are and are not willing to do.

Personally, I have a difficult time setting boundaries related to taking time for myself and can get overwhelmed and overstimulated easily. It would not be fair of me to tell my children to "go away," or my wife to "leave me alone." That would be dictating their behavior. Instead, what I could say is, "There are times when I need personal space to recharge and refresh. That requires a certain low-decibel level, and if the TV continues to be jacked to the ceiling, I'm going to have to go upstairs for some time alone." Rather than determining or mandating their behavior, this approach allows them to make a choice. They can choose to either turn the TV down and potentially continue to share space with me or continue watching the television so loudly that the neighbors three streets over can hear it, in which case I would have to remove myself from that space and they would not be able to spend time with me. By giving them this choice, I am showing them where my line is, and they get to determine whether they are going to respect that or cross it, knowing full well what will happen if that occurs.

Boundaries in Trauma Survivors

In romantic relationships, boundaries are even more important, and if that relationship has a trauma history, boundaries can sometimes feel very uncomfortable. Thinking back to previous chapters, we see a bulldozing of boundaries with fawning, codependent attunement, and other fear-based compliance. Situations that required us to do these things trained us to throw all of our boundaries out the window for personal safety. In my previous domestic violence relationship, my abuser taught me that my boundaries were not going to be respected. Boundaries related to bodily autonomy, safety, expectations of kindness… every single limit would get plowed through, and I was not able to reinforce them because reinforcement would lead to further disrespect of my boundaries and could lead to getting hurt physically, verbally, or emotionally. My ability to enforce my own personal boundaries was literally beaten out of me.

When we have parts that are afraid of getting hurt, it can then lead to difficulty in actually paying attention to what our boundaries are. Several times, I have had to be reminded that my voice matters, my time matters, and my safety matters. My wife is consistent about always reminding me how much I am allowed to say no, especially when the children are demanding of time that I don't have the energy to give, I overcommit to work tasks, or I genuinely don't want to do something. But parts of me still scream that I need to comply for fear of rejection, for fear of safety, for fear of abandonment, for fear of all these things that we have talked about, so I have to do some internal reassurance that I am safe and my needs are important.

Reestablishing boundaries after a history of trauma is incredibly difficult and a lifelong process. We are asking ourselves to turn inward and listen to what we need, all the while getting messages from these internal parts about why our needs are wrong. So we are fighting a double battle: we have to attune internally to listen to the fears of our parts and try to reassure them that they are allowed to have boundaries, *and* we have to adhere to those boundaries. So, how do we do that? Melissa Urban encourages us to use a multistep process,[35] which we will build off of throughout the concepts in this chapter. These include 1) identifying the need for the boundary, 2) setting the boundary using clear, kind language, and 3) maintaining the boundary.

Identifying the Need for the Boundary

The first step in setting a boundary is identifying the need for one. What feels safe? What feels doable? What feels wrong? Where are those lines? If you listen internally, you can usually identify them as your knee-jerk reactions (e.g., *I don't want to! I'm tired! I'm overstimulated! I'm scared! I feel unsafe!*). These reactions are typically then bulldozed by your own fear-based trauma responses (e.g., *Yes, you* can *do that! You don't* need *self-care or down time! You* have to *meet that need for your partner(s) even though it feels scary, wrong, or unsafe!*). Table 1 presents two examples of these responses in

---

[35] Melissa Urban, *The Book of Boundaries: Set the Limits That Will Set You Free* (New York: The Dial Press, 2022).

Table 1. Examples of Setting Boundaries Using PEACE TALKS.

Situation	Initial Feeling	Trauma/Fear-Based Parts	Pause	Boundary	Emotional Responses
"We need volunteers at the school. Can you help out?"	Ugh, I don't want to help. I'm burned out! I just want to hang out with my daughter at this event, not babysit a bunch of other kids!	But if you don't do this, they'll think you're a bad mom and then you'll be "that" mom who only shows up at kindergarten drop off and graduation! You'll be seen as a failure!	Pause. Breathe. Check In.	"I'm sorry. While I'm going to attend the event with my daughter, I will not be able to volunteer as a parent helper."	That was hard. That feels gross. I think they'll be mad. It's okay if they're mad. I feel good that I defended my need for my own time and my experience with my daughter.
Partner: "Let's have sex tonight!"	Nope! I'm feeling really tired and stressed. It wouldn't be good for me to push that.	But you need to do this for them. They'll be so mad and it'll start a big fight. You want to make them happy and ensure the relationship is okay!	Pause. Breathe. Check In.	"I'm not feeling great tonight, Babe. I'm really tired and wired. Would you like to snuggle and watch a movie with me instead? I'd feel comfortable doing that."	I hate disappointing them. What if they're mad? What if they want to break up?! Even though they might be mad, I'm feeling okay in my body with that boundary. I feel like I can trust myself to keep myself safe.

particular situations, along with some sample boundaries that can be set after use the PEACE approach.

We have spent a lot of time in this book learning to identify our fear-based protector responses and piece them out from the deeper feelings underneath. Setting boundaries goes a step further. Those deeper feelings underneath are true boundary-setting fodder—the good stuff—the materials from which we build the new scaffolding of what we will and will not accept in this new life. Once you are no longer in constant danger, you need to start shaping this "container" of what gets in and what stays out in order for your parts to trust that you will protect yourself.

Sometimes the idea of hard lines is really uncomfortable. So, what if we rebrand the word "boundaries"? Instead of thinking of boundaries as hard and fast restrictions, rules, or mandates, we can instead start by saying that "setting boundaries means extending courtesy to the anxious parts of ourselves." This courtesy opens a space for curiosity, and curiosity opens up lines for questioning what we "know" (e.g., *Is this me or my trauma response talking?*) It also allows space for uncertainty, for different parts to have different opinions, and for exploration of the need behind the boundary (e.g., *I want people to see me as a hard worker, but I'm tired and know I need to rest. I want to make my partner happy, but I'm also uncomfortable with being touched in that way*). We can start to notice patterns of self-sacrifice that permeate through our actions and decisions. Maybe in the past you learned that your boundaries and needs were not going to be respected, for example, and now in your current relationships your internal language mirrors those old messages. If you can extend the courtesy to explore those feelings, you can open the doors and provide some reassurance that your needs matter and self-sacrifice is not needed. By soothing and holding those scared parts, you can start to disentangle your trauma-induced desire to be silent.

When I am asked to do something that extends beyond my normal functioning (e.g., a social event, an extra work task, or cooking dinner on a day that I am worn out), I have to do an internal check-in. The question is not whether I *can* do something but whether I *want* or *should* do something. I ask myself, *Does this feel right to me?* I usually have to step back from my inherent push to say yes and really hear myself saying, "I'm tired," "I'm stressed," "I feel unseen." I don't zap these feelings away; I lean in and attune to those messages.

> **Recall a time when you pushed past your boundaries and your trauma-based parts took over. What was the outcome? What were some of the internal messages that led to that decision? What boundary could you now set to avoid this happening in the future?**

Setting Clear Boundaries

Once we identify that a situation requires a boundary, we then need to use clear, kind language that conveys exactly what we need, want, or expect. Essentially, put your *why* from the first step into words. You might need a little time to come up with just the right phrasing, which is okay as long as the situation is not threatening or scary and requires a hard STOP! Well-worded boundaries might involve others, or they may just be personal to you, such as "I need some alone time to recharge" or "I hear that you want me to process your workday with you. I'm feeling really overstimulated right now, so I'm going to go for a walk around the block. When I get back, I'd love to hear about your day." Clear boundaries provide individualized directions for those around you regarding how to interact with you, what to expect from you, and what you will not tolerate.

Boundaries are tools that allow us to stay in relationships with people in healthy ways as we redefine what we need to feel safe (after all, safety is one of the cornerstones of any and all relationships). When you set yours, do so the way we learned to apologize in the previous chapter: all meat and potatoes, but without the ZAP! Don't let your message get lost in wordiness, overexplaining, apologizing for setting the boundary, or being wishy-washy. Dig deep to remember all the things you would advocate for in your life, such as your children, animals, or injustice, then turn that advocacy inward and advocate for yourself.

Maintaining the Boundary

Okay, so you set a boundary. You looked inside and figured out what you truly needed, *and* you actually put it into words. But now your spouse gives you a pouty face, your child throws a fit, or your boss seems really disappointed. This is where the true test comes in: maintaining that boundary. And that test involves really digging in and making sure that you uphold your commitment to yourself. Once you start building confidence and trust with your parts that they can count on you to protect them, the quickest way to break that trust is to give in, blow through your boundary, and relive all those times in your past when your boundaries and needs were not respected. Respecting yourself by maintaining your boundaries is the absolute first step in getting others to respect you and, ultimately, getting your needs met.

Imagine this ultra-ridiculous scenario for a moment: Your neighbor comes over to your house, picks up your puppy, and says, "Your puppy is really cute. I've always wanted a puppy. I'm going to take yours! Sound good?" Your first instinct would be, "Heck no! That's *my* dog!" You might waffle a bit trying to determine whether they are serious. You might internally catalog through what your legal options are or figure out how you can avoid neighborhood drama, but ultimately, you will land on a hard "no." *What if he starts pouting?* Still no. *What if he kicks and screams and throws a fit?* Still no. *What if he makes threats to start rumors about me or make my life terrible?* Still a hard pass, buddy.

Maintaining your boundary despite all the possible threats, insults, emotional reactivity, and manipulation allows you to keep your puppy and honor that relationship with a little being that relies on you for care, comfort, and love. That puppy represents the younger parts of yourself that rely on you for validation, compassion, and protection. Maintaining your boundaries demonstrates to those parts that you are committed to your own safety and authenticity.

How to Accept a Boundary

Sometimes when others set boundaries, we might have some feelings about it. It may feel prohibitive or uncomfortable. It may not make sense to us. We might feel the need to get more information, have them explain the logic behind it, and in some ways "prove" to us the need for the boundary. When that happens, take a step back. Do some internal checking as to what is going on behind your resistance to their boundary. Often, we are afraid that something will upset the homeostasis and balance of our relationships, specifically by shaking up our confidence in getting our needs met. We may need to check in with ourselves to figure out what we are afraid of so that we can ask our partner(s) for reassurance and redefinition of the rules and expectations. Remember, your job is not to understand or validate the needs of others but to respect and honor them. And you can do this more readily when everyone in the relationship feels a mutual goal of safety and security.

If your partner or partners are having a difficult time accepting your boundaries, hold fast. You can provide reassurance or clarification if needed (if they ask from a place of curiosity). You can provide reminders as needed. But because boundaries are so individualized, it is up to you to establish them, reinforce them, and work to honor those of others.

Expectations and Agreements

Other forms of boundaries are expectations and agreements. When we first enter into a relationship, we typically have a series of conversations with our partner(s) about food, family, politics, and preferences (e.g., "Are you a cat or dog person?" Dog, obviously). When we have a trauma history, these early conversations might include disclosures of abuse history, family rejection, or coming out stories. Rarely do we have conversations about how often we expect to have sex, how we fight, how we expect the work/chore balance to be, or what we need to feel safe. Even writing these examples, I cringe with how vulnerable it can feel to have those conversations with someone you may have only met a few times. However, I also know how fast relationships can develop (especially queer relationships), and without some of these conversations, things can get messy quickly!

When I was first starting to date my wife after having come out of a few pretty nasty relationships, I had some knowledge about what I wanted, needed, and would not tolerate. But being the queers we are, she moved in before we really sat down to talk about how that might play out in our relationship. There were things about her that I did not realize would be difficult to navigate. She had a very physically and sexually traumatic childhood that drastically impacted her desire for physical touch and sexual intimacy. I was coming out of one relationship that significantly lacked that intimacy and another that weaponized sex. Wow, we had some chatting to do!

There were fights, hurt feelings, many "My needs are important, too" moments, and lots of tears. Sex had been so weaponized for her that it was not something she thought much about on a regular basis. Therefore, she did not initiate touch or physical intimacy in an uninhibited or carefree way. I did not understand this. To me, touching was like breathing. It was easy, carefree, and natural to me, so I would get so upset that she would not reach for me, mindlessly hold my hand, or initiate sex on a regular basis. Because of my traumatic past, I was desperate to experience physical intimacy in all the positive ways that felt good, safe, and right. Positive physical connection was my safety, and without it, I was feeling unsafe. I was getting triggered and having emotional flashbacks to times when physical touch was either withheld as a means of intentional punishment, or painful and abusive. In my mind (because of my trauma-based responses), her lack of touch meant that she did not love me or was going to hurt me. From her perspective, my desire to touch her meant that I was going to hurt her and she was not in control. We both felt unsafe—in the most safe and loving relationship either of us had ever been in.

Once we unpacked our individual *whys*, we started discussing the *hows*. Ultimately, we started having conversations that led to a better understanding of what the other person needed underneath the cacophony of noise and began setting some boundaries. She needed to feel safe. She needed to know in her bones that she had absolute physical autonomy and space and that, no matter what, she could say no at any time without consequence. Of course this was already the case, but she had been so programmed to believe that her safety did not matter that we spent (and spend) significant time providing reassurance of this fact. She needed warning when touch was going to happen and check-ins that touches were "okay." These boundaries allowed her to feel safer and trust that she was in control of her own body, and for her parts to trust that she was not going to give in or put them in positions to get hurt again.

As for me, I needed to know that she loved me, wanted me, and that our relationship was stable even if we were not having sex all the time. So, we started discussing ways that she could provide that reassurance and explore "gray areas" of physical intimacy. We discussed "safe zone" areas (hand holding, back scratching, hand on the small of the back) that felt safe to touch no matter the headspace (albeit always fully revokable if needed). Everything else (kissing, longer hugs, snuggles, sex) needed check-ins. These guidelines helped me understand that there was a method to our approach; I was not just flailing in the dark, scared and unfulfilled. Her boundaries gave me ways to keep from unintentionally triggering her (which would do more damage to our relationship and push her away further) and kept me from being chronically disappointed if my attempts to physically connect were rebuffed. We had a plan! I was able to recognize that it was not about her keeping anything from me, but about her needing to feel safe. And it was not about me getting something from her, but about me feeling connected. And, despite all the discussions, expectations, and agreements, we still fight about this at times because, trauma.

Below is my internal dialogue from the beginning of my relationship with my wife. These are unfiltered part responses that give you a glimpse into where you may be starting in your own relationship. In this example, my wife sets a clear boundary. You then see my parts struggling to sit with the discomfort that comes with a boundary that might impact my desire for relational connection. If some parts don't resonate with you, that's okay. There are still times when I have a little internal dialogue with myself, albeit with far fewer parts involved and much more compassion extended. And that is because of all the work I have done on myself and my attachment needs, as well as the deep conversations and boundary-setting my wife and I have done and continue to do as we navigate through this life together.

<u>*Digging Deeper Example: The Parts Party*</u>

(This whole sequence took about five minutes from start to finish).

Midway through sex, my wife abruptly stops and disengages. Telling me that she feels triggered and did not like something I did, she rolls over and turns out the light. Here is my resulting Parts Party in response to her boundary.

Part 1:   Oh no! What did I do! I'm so pissed at myself! I didn't know that wasn't okay!

Part 2:   I feel like this happens all the time. I didn't mean to hurt her or upset her. Now I feel sad, alone, ashamed, and really disconnected.

(I feel frustrated in the moment—frustrated with myself and with the situation. My mind starts to spiral ...)

Part 3:   Of course she can have boundaries and say no whenever she feels uncomfortable. We've talked about this and worked on this, and I encourage this all the time. It's important that she feels safe with me.

Part 4:   Am I not allowed to just be in the moment and enjoy sex? Do I have to be in my head the whole time, trying to figure out if she feels okay? Where does *my* pleasure come into play? When do *I* get to have my needs met?

(At this point I can feel my heart rate rising, myself getting really anxious and agitated, and my thoughts beginning to race. I'm mad at her!)

Part 5:   Now she's going to be distant for like a week. Ugh!

Part 6:   Oh no, maybe she doesn't find me sexually attractive anymore. I should probably ask her and make sure. Even if she says she is, maybe I'll ask her again and make her give me some examples as to why and how.

Part 7:   I hear about lesbian bed death all the time. Is this an indication? Does she want somebody else instead?

Part 8:   She does this all the time. Is she really, *really* triggered? She wouldn't use her triggers as a way to get out of having sex with me, would she? Am I really that gross?

Part 9:   That's not like her. It's not fair to think like that.

Part 10: You are such an asshole for thinking that she might do that. How dare you! She's been through hell. You're so selfish for putting your needs first and thinking that she'd ever do that to you.

(My anger and agitation are now turning inward toward shame and frustration with myself.)

Part 11:   You should probably just not initiate sex ever again. It's too scary. It's too much of a minefield. It hurts too much to get rejected.

Part 12: I should just push down my sexual attraction toward her. I shouldn't be a sexual person. Oh God, maybe she's not a sexual person. What if this never changes? I need to ask her that.

(I'm starting to panic and can feel the electricity shoot out from my chest down to my fingertips. The insistence that I feel to clarify that we are okay and that she still wants me is so intense!)

Part 13: No, I definitely don't want to talk to her about this. She already feels shame and guilt. It would just make her feel even crappier to know that I was upset and had questions. I don't want to make her take care of me.

Part 14: I really do want her to take care of me and reassure me. I need to know that it's okay. What if this is the future of our relationship? Will it always be this hard?

Part 15: It's not her job to take care of me! I worked really hard to not have that be the norm and to be able to reassure myself. I should be able to take care of my parts.

Part 16: Then what are we doing in the first place? If we're not actually going to be able to talk to each other, why are we even in a relationship? This is so dumb.

(I still feel anxiety, a full body buzz, and activation. I also feel really tired and defeated. I feel sad and angry, but I don't know who I'm angry at.)

Part 17: I'm going to roll over and go to sleep without talking to her. It's easier than saying something regrettable. It's easier than trying to figure out how vulnerable I want to be. It feels better than pushing down my own stuff to reassure her or make her push down her stuff to take care of me.

_____

_____

_____

_____

_____

_____

_____

_____

_____

_____

_____

Chapter 9

Let's Talk about Sex, Baby, and How You Can Stop "Shoulding" the Bed

*"In nature, nothing is perfect and everything is perfect.
Trees can be contorted, bent in weird ways,
and they're still beautiful."*
— Alice Walker

There is a wide variance in sexual and aromantic expression, and in the following chapter about intimacy, we will explore different ways to connect physically. This chapter focuses specifically on sex and how sexual desire, action, and interpretations can be impacted by a history of trauma.

One thing that can screw us up the most is the idea we have in our heads about how things are *supposed* to be. We know we love our partners, so things *should* be easy. Sex, intimacy, and the ability to trust and fall completely in love, lust, and desire *should* be simple.

Right?! While that might be the case with some partnerships, when it comes to relationships with people who have a traumatic past, navigating physical intimacy can be anything but easy. The messages we receive from mainstream media, friends, family, and other avenues about what sex is *supposed* to be like can be very damaging when we are trying to cozy up to our person or people.

We now understand that feelings of safety and security can be hijacked by traumatic events, especially if those events involve physical or sexual exploitation and/or aggression. So when we try to develop close relationships with our partners, parts of us are going to freak out. Those parts may emotionally push our partner(s) away, sabotage potential physical encounters, start fights, dissociate, or have internal wars. An internal war might look like wanting to please our partner, being frustrated with ourselves for having difficulty engaging in what others may see as typical, and/or having active flashbacks.

My wife, for example, often tells me that she "wants to want" me; she loves me, but she cannot "feel" it in the moment. You know, hearing that your partner cannot feel attraction or sexual desire toward you, especially when that is something you identify as vitally important to you, can *really* screw with your head. So many times I questioned the relationship longevity and wrestled with my own internal wars related to how I could be in a relationship when there were times that my partner could not feel the same connection I could feel. We had so many fights about sex. So many. It was not until we started to really unpack what we were fighting about that we were able to see beyond the issues.

Sex was a way *I* felt completely vulnerable and connected. Sex was a way *I* could feel desired, which played upon my own internal self-esteem issues. Sex was what *I* learned was typical. Because I had learned through a variety of messaging that "normal" couples have sex a certain number of times each week and that that indicates a healthy relationship connection, I felt there was something fundamentally wrong with us. But, since trauma was involved in both my and my wife's history, all those statistics had to go out the window. We had to have tough conversations about the needs behind the action and find creative approaches to get those needs met in ways that did not trigger my wife.

When I dug deep, I realized that I needed to feel desirable. I needed to be able to have a space for vulnerable connection. Guess what? Once I started listening to what *she* wanted too, I discovered we were not all that different. She wanted to have a space for vulnerable connection too, but sex was way too complicated for her to feel vulnerable. It was triggering her, making her pull away and disengage from connecting with me, which was the exact opposite of what I wanted.

So how did we both get our needs met? Once we got on the same page about what we needed, we learned we could do those things on a regular basis and in a variety of ways; it did not have to be black or white, sex or no sex. We could find the gray, get our needs met, and fight a whole lot less.

Looking a little deeper into the emotional and mental mechanics of these situations can sometimes assist in understanding the *why* so that we can further understand the *how* of making some shifts. So let's do that.

The Blueprints of Sexual Shame

Sex is such a commonly weaponized action, it is no wonder that so many of us have a complex relationship with it. When this weaponization is introduced at a young age, when we are just starting to learn basic definitions for bigger ideas like love, our concepts of and language about sex can get mucked up pretty fast.

As children, we learn quickly what will get us into trouble, what will get us rewarded, and how to differentiate "good" behavior from "bad" behavior. We start to develop a sense of worth and learn that if we are "good," we are treated well. By that logic, when we are treated well, we believe we must be doing something right, yes? What if a young child starts getting lots of attention from an older child or adult, consisting of one-on-one play dates, gifts, promises of special bonds and secret relationships? To a little kid, this attention and "being treated well" can be exciting and feel good in the moment, but it can quickly turn into acts of power, control, and grooming toward sexual abuse. Remember Nora? Her father repeatedly played on their relationship as a means of harming her. He used grooming tactics to make her believe what she was doing was a way to show love, and that confused her developing mind with skewed messages of physical responses and emotional connection.

Playing out in adult relationships, sexual abuse can still feel (and be interpreted by someone's parts) as though it is actively happening in the present if a part of someone feels that it cannot say no to a current partner and instead fawns into sexual submission. To these frozen younger parts of the traumatized individual—the parts that still believe that pleasing a partner is more important than personal safety—the current partner can even unknowingly take on the role of the perpetrator, even if they are supportive and safe. In some cases, the personal safety of one partner becomes directly dependent on the other and compliance without connection is the only option. In others, the mere arousal response can trigger feelings of negativity, danger, or flashbacks. It is no wonder our partners might pull away or start fights—they are trying to avoid being put into positions in which they have to negate their own needs of physical and/or emotional safety in order to maintain relational safety.

For most of us, the issue is a combination of *many* of these parts and how they interact with and respond to perceived threats. Where there is sexual pleasure and arousal with a current partner combined with some feelings of shame from trauma memories, there can be a stuck cycle of trauma responses. For example, the arousal and shame combined with intense love and connection to a current partner can combine with a strong sexual desire and/or an innate conditioning that pleasing a partner is the most important thing. In turn, that can combine with the fear of not pleasing the partner or resentment that one partner is putting the other in the position to have to please them, which can then lead to body disconnection, more feelings of shame, and multiple types of flashback responses… and so on. This type of of primary part-based trauma response cycle can present in a variety of ways, but under the surface, I typically hear it from clients who have not set or even discussed boundaries and therefore lack relational safety. Here are some examples:

- Maya starts kissing Susan and starts to become aroused in the present moment. Though this feels really good to Maya, it reminds her of an arousal in the past that was really bad, painful, and scary. She has a physical flashback followed by extreme physical pain, which causes her to disengage from the sexual encounter.

- Jack begins a physically intimate encounter with Sam. Things are feeling really good in the moment, but the stimulation reminds Jack of times in the past when arousal was met with scary or painful events. Though the encounter started off feeling great, Jack is feeling shame because, in his past, some things could feel physically stimulating even when someone was hurting him or touching him in ways he did not want to be touched. This makes him feel "dirty, gross, shameful" and want to pull away from his current partner. Jack has an emotional or physical flashback and instant intimacy remorse, also known as an "intimacy hangover." He withdraws from the sexual encounter and falls into a shame spiral for the rest of the day. At times, he may ask Sam for some reassurance that he is not "bad, wrong, or gross."

- Lane starts kissing Devin, clearly hoping for sexual activity. Devin's body and brain are not interested or aroused at the moment, even though he truly cares about Lane. Devin's feelings for Lane and his desire to make Lane happy conflict with his past instances when he could not say no and had to comply or else be hurt. Devin decides to move forward and have sex with Lane. His desire to make Lane happy is in the present, but it is also fueled by his fear of not making his past abusers happy. He goes through with the sexual encounter but disconnects from his body. This leads to an emotional flashback and physical numbing, but he continues having sex. Afterward, Devin avoids intimacy for the next week because he is carrying resentment toward Lane. He starts picking fights with Lane, goes into a shame spiral, and becomes really depressed.

Sexual Shame Through a Queer Lens

Extrapolating sex-based shame into the realm of queer identity and relationships is a loaded topic that could encompass an entire library of books. However, in the work I do, I often recognize primary themes. I see individuals like Hannah, whose parental rejection forced her to hide aspects of herself, including her queer identity. Her early messages of who she needed to be in order to be loved created an internalized rejection of her own sexual and romantic orientation. In so doing, this causes her to reject her identity. She hides her attraction, sexual activity, and romantic relationships from her family of origin, employers, and friends because she assumes they will reject, judge, or leave her. This plays out in relationships as Hannah being "hot and cold" with her partner(s)—she may be very loving and physical behind closed doors, but she pushes her partner(s) away either physically or emotionally when in public or when they are triggered by internalized homophobia.

Triggers

Trauma impacts so many different aspects of a person, but physical and/or sexual trauma comes with a fallout that impacts one of the most basic forms of relational connection: sex and physical intimacy. With trauma comes triggers. So what is a partner responsible for mitigating beforehand, and why is it important to know how to respond after the fact?

Recognizing that we can keep our partner(s) feeling safe by avoiding specific words or phrases or certain kinds of touch helps us prevent unnecessary physical or emotional triggers. Paying attention to our actions, where we are putting our hands, or the words we are using can play a vital role in helping create an environment of safety. I have worked with clients who could not have their partners say "I love you" during sex because it was a phrase used by their perpetrators. In one scenario, a client could not allow their partners to remove the client's clothes—the client needed to do it themselves—because perpetrators took that freedom away from them in the past. Another client needed to hear that they were loved no matter what before engaging in any sexual activity because their perpetrator would make them feel like they would never be loved or wanted if they did not engage in sexual activity. If our partners know that we genuinely care about them feeling safe, if we truly invest in their story, they are far more likely to build trust in our intentions, feel confident in their ability to say no if needed, and lean into physical vulnerability.

Responding to Trauma-Based Responses of Our Partners

Even in the best-case scenarios, we cannot control *every* potential for a trigger response, because sometimes our partner does not know what might be triggering in any one particular moment. Because of this, we need to know how to respond when it happens.

The first thing we need to do is recognize what is happening and pump the brakes. If you are in the middle of something, stop. Check in with your partner to make sure they are grounded in the here and now. Reassure them that they are safe. If they are not in the present, see if you can help them return to their adult self in the present using your coregulation skills.

After taking a step back, we then need to ask our partners what they need to feel safe. Sometimes it will be physical space, sometimes verbal reassurance, and other times grounding and eye contact might be all it takes. Sometimes your partner(s) may be nonverbal. It varies from person to person and from minute to minute. Just remember to be patient with them. You can ask simple yes or no questions to make it easier for them, but, due to their nervous system being activated, their frontal lobe will not be accessible, so they likely will not be able to access meaningful language or immediately process the event or trigger.

Once we have learned what our partners need, the final step is to *believe* them. If your partner says they need space, believe that they genuinely need space and give it to them. If they assure you that they are okay and want to continue, you are giving them autonomy over their body and helping them believe that you trust them and that they can trust you. Give them permission to stop if needed, and reassure them that you will not be angry with them for needing this.

The overall rule when it comes to responding to your partner's trauma-based responses is that *it is not about you.* This is the crux of any immediate supportive reaction. If the person sitting next to you were to get shot, you would rush to their aid to make sure they are okay. You would not ask them why they had the audacity to get in the way of the bullet or bemoan about how they needed medical attention. The time to support and stabilize your partner is when they are first triggered. You will get a chance to unpack feelings of rejection or frustration at a later moment. This prioritization of your partner can be frustrating for some parts of you, which is understandable. However, your being able to provide support in these moments will not only benefit your partner instantaneously but also build a foundation of safety that will enhance and strengthen your relationship with them overall.

Boundaries

Ideally, each individual has the ability to say yes or no, stop or go, more or less. However, our partners may not have been given the freedom to voice those boundaries, and even if they did, they might not have been respected. Because of this, we need to encourage our partners to be as vocal as possible. You can say, for example, "Tell me when you're unsure, something doesn't feel right, or something feels good but deep down there's another feeling of guilt or shame." Then you need to make space to hear it all—without judgment or taking it personally. Yes, this is hard, especially when you just want to connect and get out of your head. However, in doing this, you are helping your partner(s) develop internal self-trust.

Someone who has experienced grooming was taught to ignore internal feelings of pain, accept advances without question (regardless of internal screams of "no!"), and push down their own comfort because the risk to their safety was too great. Because of this, we have to take a step back and create a safe space where they can reclaim themselves before they can give themselves over in an intimate way. If we move too fast, we can risk our partners disengaging emotionally, ignoring internal protests, and even replaying those learned obligatory roles of pleasing us to avoid the risk of pain or rejection. This is a long, hard, and fluid process. You will likely have countless internal protests of your own related to your needs for connection, feeling rejected, and feeling like you are putting your partner's needs above your own. And, for a time, you might be.

There have been times when I wanted to connect with my wife, but she was trying to listen to her body and respect her internal boundaries. Like the Parts Party I shared with you in the previous chapter, I would feel rejected or abandoned and then get angry and yell about my need to feel safe as well (which included physical connection). I would leave the room, convinced that "it wasn't fair" and that I had to "always meet her needs instead of her meeting mine!" I would cite the love languages, explaining that if she "really loved me" she would find ways to connect with me. I was wrought with desperation and incredulousness. Even typing that makes me cringe. But cringy or not, it was true and felt very real in the moment. A part of me felt frantic to connect because I had been in relationships in which sex had either been weaponized or withheld for purposes of intentional manipulation. Some part of me interpreted her unwillingness to kiss me or touch me as dancing on that triggered nerve of rejection and, damnit, I needed relational safety!

Consequently, I needed to do some deep internal work into why I felt the rejection, why I was so desperate for connection, and why some parts of me were so frustrated that I felt that "her needs always won." A little clue: it is not the trauma Olympics. There are no winners. But for some reason, I always felt that sting of a silver medal when the topic of sex came up. I felt that we were not "okay" if we were not having sex on a regular basis. If she loved me, I thought, she *should* want to have sex. If we were meant to be together, this *should* be easy! I was "shoulding" the bed.

Once my wife and I started to do more unpacking, we were able to get to the heart of the issue: the need for relational safety is less important than the need for physical safety in the body. Period. You cannot have relational safety when you do not feel safe in your body. Therefore, if I wanted to get my needs of relational safety met, I had to make damn sure she felt safe in her body first.

How did we do that?

I needed to give her space. I needed to trust her. At first, it was more like limp along, mess up, do better, argue with myself, argue with her, cry, try harder, and so on, and so on. This is how navigating trauma works. It is not easy. It is messy. Really messy!

Eventually, though, we started seeing some shifts in how we interacted with each other. We recognized that we both wanted the same thing: to feel safe and loved. While we had different definitions of what these words meant for both of us, we could agree that we wanted to discover more about how to feel them *and* how to help each other feel them, too.

On my wife's end, she needed to start noticing things. Like many of the things we have discussed in this book, this starts in a reactive way. She would notice, for example, that after sex she felt depressed, anxious, or shameful. We made space for that, and I tried my damnedest not to make it about me or get caught up in the guilt spiral of *What did I do to make her feel that way? How could I have prevented it? How did I not know it was hard for her?* There were times I would not initiate sex or physical touch of any kind so that I could avoid triggering her and because I did not want her to have to wrestle with whether she felt safe. After all, not initiating would mean guaranteed safety, right? Nope. My lack of initiation was interpreted by her as my assuming that she was "too broken" or "too fragile" or that I was taking away an opportunity for her to make her own decision about her body. So, celibacy was not the answer, either (thank goodness, because that would not have worked for me long term). There were times I resented the hell out of her because I would intentionally not initiate for weeks. While I saw this as a great sacrifice on my part, she did not even notice, because sex is not something that naturally or regularly enters her stream of consciousness. So, we settled on trial and error, and she focused on noticing. The reactive noticing of the "aftereffects" started to develop into more in-the-moment noticing and practicing saying no, even if she did not know why.

On my end, I helped by continuously reminding her of the importance of self-trust in terms of not compromising her boundaries—even when I was disappointed or hurt. I had to provide reassurance that she could say no *at any time* and that I would respect that boundary. I had to reassure her that she was not "in trouble" and that I would not be mad or leave her if she set a boundary. This communication started to develop into a mutual trust. Because she could trust that I would always stop and reassure her, she started to trust herself to be more vocal about her needs. Being more vocal about her needs then led to better communication about what was safe or unsafe, good or bad, which led to more physical intimacy and safe expression of physical love. She started to do prevention check-ins with all of her parts before physical intimacy, which sometimes prevented unnecessary triggering or rejection. If there was any inkling of something kickstarting, she would check in to make sure things felt safe and right and that there were no objections or feelings of obligation that might derail things. All the while she knew that even if things were "good to go" at the onset, at any time during, she still had the safety of saying no.

Finding the Gray

The idea of deviation from the heteronormative sexual encounter should not be rocket science for us queer folk, but sometimes we can still have the gendered programming that feels like sex is not "real sex" unless we get around *all* the bases. We have to ask ourselves what it is we *really* want and need. If the answer is a movie-star, earth-shattering, simultaneous-orgasms-every-time-we-walk-into-the-same-room relationship, sorry, friends, but that "shoulding" is likely to really stink up your love life. Adding pressure to sexual encounters will not help. At all. In fact, it will likely push away your partner even more because their level of expectation for performance may feel too similar to past situations when no was not an option. That expectation can look like birthday and anniversary celebrations, date nights without the kids, or even you walking into the bedroom with a sexy outfit on. The feelings of *I have to do this because my partner is expecting it and I love my partner* can threaten to undo their internal cues for safety, which can lead to instances when your partner feels more pressure to say yes and hurt themselves than say no and risk disappointing you. Being aware of this and vocalizing that there are "no expectations" (and meaning it!), will be essential for navigating through those times of expectation.

To celebrate all the bases with equal merit, our partner(s) need to believe that we will be content with a single or a double and that any kiss or sensual touch will not automatically be assumed as rounding third and heading for home plate. This can be a tough adjustment at first, because sometimes we are so excited that our partner is showing interest that we want to race to the finish line. I can tell you from personal experience that this race does not always end well. Sometimes it can make partners nervous to express desire, for fear that it will be assumed they need to perform.

Another way to navigate this is by figuring out what we really *need* from physical contact. Maybe what we really want is connection, to feel desired, or to feel like we are seen. Those things can still happen and in a satisfying way. Start with vocalizing the need: "Babe, I am really needing some kind of connection. Do you have the space for that?" This allows your partner to do internal check-ins to see what feels safe and what they can give. Maybe they will give you a big kiss or hug. Maybe they will respond with, "Of course! I'd love it if we could snuggle on the couch. How does that sound?" Or maybe they will say, "Baby, I love you so much and I know you need connection, but I had a really hard day today and am not feeling super touchy. Could we watch a show together or go for a walk together instead?" No .matter the response, this dialogue allows exploration of the "gray area" of physical intimacy, the area where everyone involved feels safe and nourished. It also allows your survivor-partner to explore different kinds of physical expression and sexuality.

Digging Deeper Activity

What are some ways you feel physically connected to your partner(s)? Are there areas where you or they have difficulty? Areas where there is disconnect (either in drive, desire, initiation, or activity)? What are some "grey areas" that you could explore together? Do some internal self-exploration around the messages you receive about sex and physical touch. Are there any messages that you see playing out in your past or current relationships? Any triggers that you have not explored with your partner(s)? How might you use PEACE TALKS skills to explore those internally and then present them to your partner?

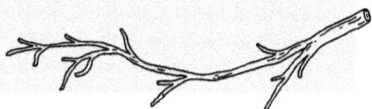

_____

_____

_____

_____

_____

_____

_____

_____

_____

Chapter 10
Connection: Intimacy and Vulnerability

The roots of education are bitter,
but the fruit is sweet.
– Aristotle

The topic of intimacy is about more than just the way we give and receive love. It has greater depth. Throughout the book, we have talked about attachment in terms of understanding lack of safety in previous relationships and developing safety in current ones. However, attachment and intimacy differ. Attachment focuses on basic trust and whether you can count on your partner. It is the "What will you do that will either hurt me or protect me?" safety; the you *for* me safety. Intimacy is a dynamic that builds on attachment and takes it a step further. It is a mutual meeting of support and needs that involves having compassion and giving and holding that space in a way that celebrates differences and encourages growth. You don't have to be matched perfectly in all areas with your partner(s), but you do need to have conversations about your needs, the ways that you feel loved, the ways that you like to express love, and why you need those things (which can be learned and/or programmed). Ultimately, to have true intimacy, you have to know what your goals are as a couple or partnership.

In my experience as a therapist, I have seen queer partners be more comfortable with discussions around intimacy, even at the very beginning of their relationships. Because boundaries are integrated into queer relationships as an assumptive part of the partnering process, it can sometimes be easier to branch into conversations about the different kinds of intimacy, getting different needs met by different people, and the idea that one size does not fit all. However, not everyone is wired this way. Due to a variety of factors such as indoctrination, heteronormativity, and media messaging, these discussions might still lead to difficult realizations and internal conflict. Likewise, in relationships in which one or more partners have a history of trauma, trust and vulnerability are two areas that are some of the most difficult to establish in a comfortable way. To assist in diving into these discussions about intimacy, we can consider the different types of intimacy and how communication, attachment, and boundaries play their roles.

- **Physical and Sexual Intimacy**
  When discussing intimacy, the first thing that initially comes to mind is typically physical and sexual intimacy. While all sex is intimate, not all intimacy equals sex. Because of this, we need to explore the vastness of physical intimacy in all its forms and ways of being communicated, felt, and experienced. Physical intimacy can be anything from a loving touch to kissing, sex, and everything in between. The key is to explore and communicate. Discuss with your partner what feels good, safe, and exciting.

- **Emotional Intimacy**

  Emotional intimacy allows for the giving and receiving of different emotions in attempts to build trust and create strong relational foundations. Sharing that honesty and vulnerability is what leads to emotional closeness, or that feeling of "I can count on you, and you can count on me to handle the hard stuff." In relationships that have one or more partners with a trauma history, emotional intimacy is necessary, but can also be quite difficult. Because traumatic histories include issues with attachment and historically not getting emotional needs met, it can be incredibly difficult for such partners to trust their emotional needs in the hands of their partner. Developing patient awareness and compassion can assist in building trust through consistency.

- **Intellectual Intimacy**

  Intellectual intimacy involves sharing thoughts and opinions and having those respected by your partner. It allows for a safe space in which to process anything from politics to the most recent gluten-free muffin recipe. With intellectual intimacy comes a safeness to explore and stretch each other's knowledge, awareness, humility, and even things like deeply held biases.

- **Spiritual Intimacy**

  Spiritual intimacy does not necessarily have to involve religion, but can include topics of spirituality and those big life questions about meaning, purpose, and the afterlife. One major facet of spiritual intimacy is that we don't have to agree in order to exchange respect. We can be curious and want to learn about our partners' existence and experiences, not for the purposes of validation or convincing, but for purposes of witnessing and hearing each other, deepening our connection through mutual respect for our differences.

- **Experiential and Shared-Life Intimacy**

  The intimacy that comes through experiential knowledge and sharing each other's lives includes themes of commitment toward shared goals, whether that involves family dynamics, household chores, money and financial issues, managing the most recent crisis, or participating in day-to-day and bucket-list activities. Being creative together and working well together can be combined in this category as well. Knowing that you can depend on your partner to pick up the children or take the car for a tune up when you are busy at work is the kind of relational reliability that is found in this category of intimacy.

Experiencing the various types of intimacy helps strengthen the bond with our partners and creates feelings of connectedness. While not every relationship will have a "10 out of 10" rating in all of these areas of intimacy, it is important to find whatever balance works for you and your partner. Sometimes you might discuss these areas and realize that your partner is not as into WWE as you are, and you will have to get that experiential need met with someone else. Maybe your partner is a deep person who really needs to talk about the meaning of life and where we go when we die, but talking about death freaks you out. You must come to an understanding with your partner about getting those needs met through other avenues, and everyone in the relationship needs to be on board with that plan with common goals, understandings, and relational boundaries.

Where I run into issues with this as a therapist is when I see one partner wanting the other to fulfill a category of intimacy, but are mismatched in that area. Meredith, for example, desperately wants Sharon to accompany her to church and talk about the afterlife, while Sharon does not believe in organized religion and sets boundaries related to her participation. Though Sharon and Meredith have different goals and beliefs, they can still arrive at a level of spiritual intimacy. They can discuss their beliefs, respect one another's views, listen, and lean in, simply because they are each interested in understanding how the other person thinks. They don't have to convince or change each other's minds, nor do they need to understand individually before they can support each other. By establishing this conversation and mutual understanding, they can develop ways for Meredith to get her spiritual buddy needs met by asking her friend Rachel to accompany her to church. Sharon will support Meredith in this connection with Rachel because she recognizes that Meredith values spiritual connection with other individuals and inviting Rachel is not a threat to the foundation of their relationship. Sharon is able to maintain her boundary of not involving herself in organized religious practices.

Intimacy Takeaways

There are no preset rules related to intimacy. If our goal is meaningful connection, we cannot assume to know the emotions, needs, or relational priorities of others. Communication is vital. Mutual respect for maintaining the relational foundation is required. We have to get curious and ask, and then believe and respect each other's experiences. We need to be learners, not knowers. We don't have to have the same needs in order to respect our partners' needs; we have to find a balance, and every single relationship is unique.

Digging Deeper: Exploring Intimacy

1) In the areas of intimacy, what does your relationship look like now? What would you like it to look like?

   Physical: _____

   Emotional: _____

   Intellectual: _____

   Spiritual: _____

   Experiential and Shared-Life: _____

2) Is your partner capable of meeting you where you feel your needs are? If so, how can you tell them what you need and what the relational need is?

   _____

3) If your partner is not capable of meeting your needs, what could you say to start a conversation about that?

   _____

4) Are there any boundaries that need to be redefined or expressed in your relationship?

   _____

Chapter 11
Putting It All Together

*"A tree lives on its roots. If you change the root,
you change the tree. Culture lives in human beings.
If you change the human heart, the culture will follow."*
— Jane Hirshfield

Differentiating between "getting it right" and "being right" is a constant learning process. "Being right" insinuates that someone else is "wrong," in which case there would be a clear "winner" and "loser." In relationships, we instead want to get it right by working toward making the *relationship* the "winner." This is a team sport. Your partner is on your team, and there is no MVP. You work together through difficult conversations, realizations, power dynamics, bonding through trauma, and fight cycles. You both reestablish boundaries, understand what feels good in each other's bodies, and identify relational needs so you can work on fulfilling those together. In this process, you *will* trip and fall, yell and walk out, shut down and cry, because this is not a one-and-done kind of thing. This is a redefining of deeply held survival mechanisms and body-based responses. It is a relearning of how to trust, how to count on someone else when you need to, and how to learn new languages and debunk old patterns. This type of recalibration takes time.

Takeaway Tips

Remember the 70/30 Rule

In the 1950s, Dr. Donald Winnicott coined the phrase "good enough parenting" while conducting research on mothers and their babies. He indicated that we need to be fully attuned and respond well only 30 percent of the time to be able to establish good, secure attachments.[36] Though Winnicott's studies focused on only parent–child relationships, his findings can be extrapolated to partner relationships as well. So much of our attachment and stability is found in the other 70 percent, which includes the repair work *after* a triggering event, a part response, or a big feeling that impedes our ability to respond perfectly in the moment. If we responded perfectly all the time (which is not likely or healthy), we would never give our partners time to feel distress, notice those feelings, and have the space to self-soothe. In addition, because there would be constant sheltering, our partners would never push beyond the boundaries of their comfort zones, and they definitely would not trust that if they tried something new, we would be there to catch them if they fell. If we attended to our partners all the time, we would never have any time or space for ourselves, and we are equally important and complex.

---

[36] Donald W. Winnicott, "The Theory of the Parent-Infant Relationship," *International Journal of Psychoanalysis* 41 (1960): 585–595, PMID: 13785877, https://tcf-website-media-library.s3.eu-west-2.amazonaws.com/wp-content/uploads/2021/09/21095241/Winnicott-D.-1960.-The-Theory-of-the-Parent-Infant-Relationship.-International-Journal-of-Psycho-Analysis.-411.-pp.585-595-1.pdf.

This is all to say that in relationships, especially those among partners with a trauma history, there is no expectation of perfection!

Remind Yourself What You Want to Bring to "the Bonfire"

You are now more aware of how you respond, how your partner(s) responds, and what to add to or take away from fights. You know more about boundaries and how to gauge whether you have the emotional energy to coregulate or need to walk away and take space. You know that responding with your own insecurities without "Self-led" energy will lead to blame, shame, agitation, and reliving old wounds from the past. So, when your partner comes to you with their own fire burning, take this awareness and ask yourself, "What do I want to bring to the bonfire?"

Sometimes, despite your best efforts or awareness, you will bring gasoline (as seen in Figure 11). Things may escalate, tension will be high, and there may be use of "always" and "never" combined with anything *but* the eight Cs. Refer back to the 70/30 rule and extend yourself some grace in knowing that none of us gets it right all the time and that even though you did not want to get into a fight, you did. Remember all the reasons *why* you did: the part-dances, the push and pull of you and your partner's parts, and your individual and relational attachment styles and connection needs. Check in with yourself and your partner to see who was driving the bus. Use PEACE TALKS to repair.

There will also be times when you will bring *space* or *air* to the fire. You may not have the emotional energy to coregulate your partner, and pushing beyond that limit (overextending yourself) will bring resentment and frustration. Responding with the intention of calming them down means that you have a vested interest in their calm: "Calm down so I don't have to give you any more of me."

We know this sets us up for disaster because sometimes our partner(s) don't respond the way we hope and then we get mad or hurt. So, if you don't have the capacity to give for the singular purpose of giving—without expectation or vested self-interest—then walk away.

Sometimes, though you may want to provide reassurance that you hear your partner, that you care for them deeply, and that you want to be there for them in the way that they want you to be, you will not have that energy to give. In these cases, you can say something like, "I see that you're hurting. Everything feels hard right now. I want to be able to listen and show up with my whole self, but I'm super burned out. I need to take a little space and recharge, because listening and really hearing you is important, and I can't do that right now." With this approach, your partner may feel momentarily rejected or upset, but you will be able to reach those parts that really want connection and to feel heard by letting them know that being 100 percent present is a priority to you both and that you just need to take some space so you can come back as your best self.

There will be times when you have the ability to access your adult self (feel personally regulated) and can really show up and hold space for your partner by way of coregulation. Lean in and validate their experience. Sit with them by the fire, close enough that you can feel the heat but not fall in yourself, and not so far away that you are disconnected and cannot appreciate the depth of their distress.

Digging Deeper:

When is a time you can remember doing all these things (Pouring gasoline? Giving space? Or sitting beside the fire with your partner(s)?) What was the response you received? What can you "set down" for a few moments while you wait for the winds to shift and the charge to dissipate?

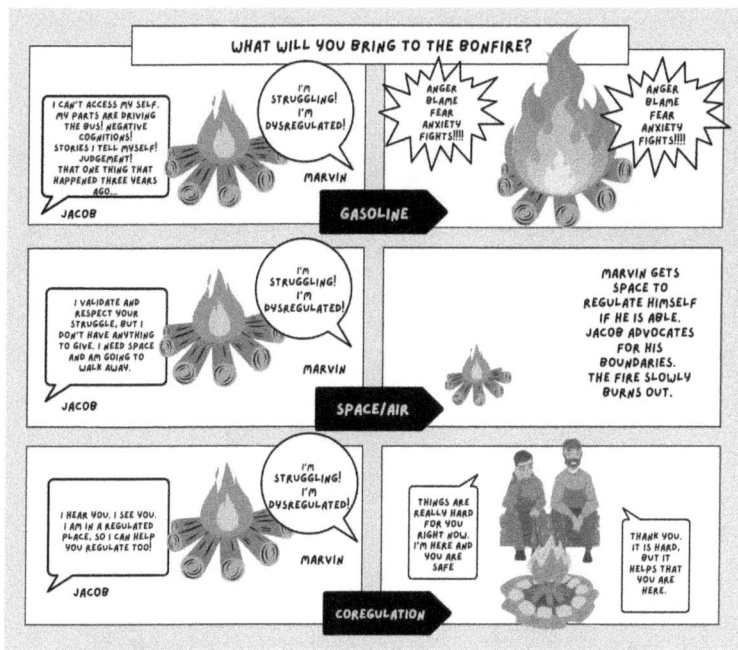

Figure 11. Partners and Their Parts at the Bonfire.

Get a Therapist

To reiterate, this book is not meant to be a substitute for your own therapy or relationship counseling. This is a personally and professionally informed guide to help you identify patterns individually and relationally so that you can take deeper dives and start channeling your energy in helpful directions. My call to action is that you seek therapy to help you process some of the hard stuff that might have come up for you while reading this book. Trauma is not a light and fluffy topic, so some professional navigation that you can actually interact with might be really beneficial. Personally, I recommend internal family systems (IFS)/ego state interventions, eye movement desensitization and reprocessing (EMDR) therapy, trauma-informed stabilization treatment (TIST), or somatic experiencing therapy, but you have to find the right fit for you. I have included some fantastic resources in the Reader Resources section at the end of this book.

Extend Grace and Compassion

Throughout our discussions, we have explored how to look at our partners through new eyes, rebrand "behaviors" as "connection" and "safety seeking," and do some repair work after blowups. Extend yourself that same grace. You are doing hard things and showing up daily to keep trying to navigate difficult dynamics because you deeply care about your partner(s). Finding compassion for yourself and having grace are vital, overarching parts of the process that cannot be overlooked.

Don't Forget the "Zhuzh"

All this information may seem like a crap-ton of work and feel utterly exhausting at times. Don't forget why you are here: to find the joy, fun, silliness, and magic in your relationship. Knowing the steps to the dance is not enough and can feel empty without the je ne sais quoi of "soulmates," "magic," "connection," or "in love" feelings. That is the glue that fills the cracks in the scaffolding of all these steps and guides. You can teach someone the steps to the dance, but unless you *feel* it (in whatever way you define it or understand it), it can fall flat. So, in all your tips, tricks, and guides, don't forget the zhuzh.

Seek and Find Ways to Feel Real and Safe

In Dr. Becky Kennedy's recent work with parenting,[37] she mentions concepts related to children needing to feel *real* and *safe* in order to

---

[37] Becky Kennedy, Good Inside: A Guide to Becoming the Parent You Want to Be (New York: Harper Collins Publishers, 2022).

feel emotionally validated and witnessed by parents. This applies to any and all relationships and transcends into our place in the world as queer individuals. Are you real? Are you safe? Feeling real might relate to your place in society and being treated as a real human, with full legal rights to marriage, adoption, parentage, health care, and benefits. Are your rights being protected? Are *you* being protected? This lack of protection can impact our internal feelings of worth—and cause us to ask ourselves if society even deems us worthy of protecting—of safety. If we're not worthy of laws and regulations reflecting our worth and safety, keeping our basic levels of protection intact, then we are more vulnerable to get those things that we love most stripped away from us. Therefore, your relationship with your partners and your community are sacred. Seek and find ways to feel safe and protected. Continue to protect others and fight for whatever drives you. Treat those in relationships with you with that same passion of noticing and witnessing. Practice ways to feel real and safe within your own body and within whatever family you have built. I see you; you are real.

Remember that relationships are hard. They are messy. They ebb and they flow. But that is because they are *alive*. And as with anything alive, you cannot just set it aside and forget about it or it will end up mummified on your office shelf (like all the plants I kill on a regular basis). You must continue to show up and try. By doing this work, you are showing up. You are showing up for your partner, for yourself, and for your relationship. Continue to embrace the vitality. Protect it, cherish it, lean in, and keep moving forward in this beautifully messy life. You can do this. I believe in you, because you are worth believing in.

Appendix

Symptoms of PTSD[38]

1) You have been exposed to a traumatic event in which both of the following were present: You experienced, witnessed, or were confronted with an event or events that involved actual or threatened death or serious injury; or you experienced, witnessed, or were confronted with a threat to the physical integrity of yourself or others.

2) Your response involves intense fear, helplessness, or horror, or your perception of the event led to these emotions.

3) You reexperience the event in one or more of the following ways:
   a) You have recurrent and intrusive distressing recollections of the event, including images, thoughts, or perceptions.
   b) You have recurrent distressing dreams of the event.
   c) You act or feel as if the traumatic event were recurring, and you may have a sense of reliving the experience through illusions, hallucinations, and/or active flashbacks.

---

[38] Adapted from American Psychiatric Association, DSM-5 Task Force, *Diagnostic and Statistical Manual (DSM-5)*, 5th ed. (New York: American Psychiatric Association, 2013).

d) You experience intense psychological distress or bodily reactions when exposed to internal or external cues that symbolize or resemble an aspect of the traumatic event (e.g., sights, smells, sounds, dates); these are called triggers.

4) You persistently avoid things or events (triggers) associated with the trauma and numb your response using three or more of the following:

a) You make a great effort to avoid thoughts, feelings, or conversations associated with the trauma, and/or you avoid activities, places, or people that would cause you to remember the trauma.

b) You cannot recall an important aspect of the trauma.

c) Your interest or participation in activities is much less than usual.

d) You feel detached or estranged from others.

e) Your ability to feel emotion is restricted, as is your range of emotions (e.g., You are unable to have loving feelings).

f) You have a sense of a foreshortened future, meaning you cannot see ahead into a far-off future (e.g., You don't expect to have a career, marriage, children, or a normal life span).

5) You have persistent symptoms of increased physical arousal that were not present before the trauma, as indicated by two or more of the following:

a) Difficulty falling or staying asleep

b) Irritability or outbursts of anger

c) Difficulty concentrating

d) Hypervigilance (being overly watchful)

e) Exaggerated startle response (jumpy)

6) The above symptoms have lasted more than one month.

7) Because of these symptoms, you are significantly distressed or
   impaired in social, occupational, or other important areas of
   functioning.

Symptoms of CPTSD

You are more likely to experience symptoms of CPTSD if your traumatization occurred early in your life, was prolonged, and was interpersonal. In addition to the PTSD symptoms above, you may have
the long-term symptoms below, which are secondary to *totalitarian
control*. According to Judith Herman, the seven symptom groups of
CPTSD include those below:[39]

Category 1: Alterations in regulation of affect (emotion) and impulses
- Chronic affect dysregulation (your emotions have a life of
  their own)
- Difficulty modulating (managing and regulating) anger
- Self-destructive or suicidal behaviors
- Difficulty modulating sexual involvement
- Impulsive and risk-taking behaviors

Category 2: Alterations in attention or consciousness
- Amnesia
- Transient dissociative episodes (short periods of zoning out)
- Depersonalization

Category 3: Somatization (how your body holds your trauma)
- Digestive system problems
- Chronic pain

---

[39] Herman, *Trauma and Recovery*.

- Cardiopulmonary symptoms
- Conversion symptoms (psychological problems that get converted into physical symptoms, such as when physical abuse as a child leads to unexplained symptoms as an adult [e.g., a child who has been hit on their back with a bat ends up having unexplained back spasms as an adult])
- Sexual symptoms
- Panic

Category 4: Alterations in self-perception (how you see yourself)
- Chronic guilt, shame, and self-blame
- Feeling that you are permanently damaged
- Feeling ineffective
- Feeling nobody understands you
- Minimizing the importance of the traumatic events in your life

Category 5: Alterations in perception of the perpetrator (this is not needed for a diagnosis of CPTSD)
- Adopting the distorted beliefs of the perpetrator about yourself, others, and what happened as true
- Idealizing of the perpetrator
- Preoccupation with hurting the perpetrator

Category 6: Alterations in relations with others
- Inability to trust
- Revictimizing yourself
- Victimizing others

Category 7: Alterations in systems of meaning (how you see life, others, and spirituality)

- Despair, hopelessness
- Loss of beliefs that previously sustained you

Book Club Discussion Questions

1. What are your main traumas that you can identify? What planted the seeds of your traumatic responses to these traumas?

2. What are your "roots" (those beliefs about yourself and the world that resulted from the trauma)?

3. What are your "leaves" (the everyday physical or emotional symptoms that you notice)?

4. What attachment style resonates with you the most? If you want to, head over to https://www.attachmentproject.com/attachment-style-quiz to explore this further.

5. Thinking back to your previous relationships, was there a way you typically responded when you felt vulnerable? Did you pull away? Did you rush toward your partner? Did the foundation of your relationship feel really shaky any time there was conflict? Where did that fear come from? Was there a person in your history you could not rely on for nurturing, safety, or connection?

6. What are some ways your current partner supports you? Nurtures you? Shows up for you? When you are feeling vulnerable, do you end up pushing your partner away instead of getting your needs for connection met? Even though it feels scary, how

might your partner respond if you leaned into the vulnerability and told them you were having a difficult time?

7. What negative cognition folders can you identify? Are there any stories you tell yourself often? Where did these come from? Can you identify when the folder was created? Are you able to challenge any of these negative cognitions with some "reality checking" from your adult life?

8. What do you think about parts? Can you identify a time when your manager part was "driving the bus"? What did this look like or feel like? How did you feel the energy or your body shift when you got your adult Self back online?

9. What are some primary ways that you can shift back into a more adult self-awareness? Is there anything you can identify that makes you happy or brings you peace? Make a list and share it with another person.

10. Can you identify a time in your life when you were over-performing (taking on too much in a relationship) because you wanted to keep the peace, get your needs met, or could not trust the other person or people to share the responsibility of the relationship work? What was your experience with this? How did it end?

11. How could you use PEACE TALKS in your everyday life? With partners? Coworkers? Children? What element of the PEACE TALKS process might be the most difficult for you and why? What might come naturally?

12. Think of a boundary you would like to establish with a partner, family member, or coworker. How might you do that? What might you say? How could you maintain the boundary regardless of pushback?

13. What are the primary ways you feel close to your partner (either current or past)? Looking at the various types of intimacy, how could you explore ways to feel more connected in your current relationship?

14. What are some ways you could make sure you are being mindful of what you are bringing to the bonfire?

Glossary

affect dysregulation: feeling out of control of one's mood or emotions

allostasis: the process by which the body responds to stressors in order to regain stability

amygdala: the brain's alarm center that scans the environment for sensory input

attachment: relational component relating to the belief that one individual will keep another safe by consistently attending to their emotional needs

attachment injury: a traumatic relational event or interaction that impacts belief in emotional or physical safety toward another person

attachment trauma: a trauma that impacts attachment at a critical developmental stage

attunement: paying attention, recognizing, and responding to a partner's emotional state

autonomic nervous system: a component of the central nervous system that regulates involuntary physiologic processes including heart rate, blood pressure, respiration, and digestion and is responsible for fight/flight/freeze mode activation

betrayal blindness: involuntarily forgetting or minimizing of trauma in current situation to maintain stability of relationship

boundary: guideline to assist in establishing and maintaining safety and relational expectations

codependence: an emotional state that is disproportionately impacted by another's emotional state

codependent attunement: being so attuned to a partner that one tries to proactively manage a partner's mood in an attempt to also calm themselves

connection of activation: feeling bonded to another due to shared stressor or trauma

coregulation: using your own regulated body, voice, and energy to assist in calming the distress of a partner

CPTSD: complex post-traumatic stress disorder

ego states: parts of the psyche that step in to assist with the various roles one has throughout life

emotional flashbacks: when the amygdala recognizes a relational trigger

enmeshment: becoming emotionally dependent and entangled with a partner

epigenetics: the study of how behaviors and environment can cause changes that affect the way one's genes work

fawn response/fawning: proactive or reactive responses in which an individual disconnects from their own emotions, sensations, and needs in order to meet the needs of others and maintain safety

hippocampus: the part of the brain where emotional memory is stored

intersectional identity: an individual's identity that is comprised of many identifying factors, including race, ethnicity, gender identity/expression, sexual identity/expression, etc.

negative cognitions: negative belief about self, others, or the world that is established through seminal/developmental events

neuroception: interpretation of internal and external cues for determining safety

parts: similar to ego states, parts are elements of the psyche that step in to assist with the various roles one has throughout life

prefrontal cortex: the part of the brain responsible for higher-level thinking, rational processing, and language formation

preventative protector part: a part that will mitigate stressors to prevent one from feeling deep pain, triggers, or activation

protector parts: parts of the psyche that step in to prevent or respond to unwanted emotional reactivity

PTSD: post-traumatic stress disorder

reactive protector part: a part that responds after the person feels pain, triggers, or activation to dismiss, bury, or evade maintaining that level of activation

repair work: intentional conversations and connections with the purpose of identifying and fixing attachment injuries and relational wounds

relational trigger: something that emotionally feels like a scary experience from the past

resiliency: internal confidence that one can traverse difficult situations because of past adversity and access to social supports and resources

Self: an adult part/higher power/inner knowing that holds the key to calm, compassionate, curious exploration of external and internal events

self concept: the way an individual thinks about themselves and views their worth in relation to the world

the eight Cs: compassion, creativity, curiosity, confidence, courage, calm, connectedness, clarity

totalitarian control: total control over another person by way of oppression, experienced or threatened violence, or manipulation.

trauma: an event or the aftermath of an event that overwhelms one's internal ability to cope

trauma memory: the way that memories are stored during a trauma, focusing on emotions and sensations versus chronological order

trigger: psychological, sensory, or emotional stimulus that prompts involuntary recall of a previous traumatic experience

unblending: recognizing when a part is responding versus an adult self and intentionally separating from that part to gain clarity

ventral vagal state: a physical state which allows connection, rest, and assists in resuming normal body functions after activation

window of tolerance: the body and brain's window where access to the prefrontal cortex is still relatively available and is not in fight/flight/freeze mode

Bibliography

Ainsworth, Mary D. Salter. "Attachments and Other Affectional Bonds Across the Life Cycle." In *Attachment Across the Life Cycle*, edited by Colin Murray Parkes, Joan Stevenson-Hinde, and Peter Marris, 33–51. London: Routledge, 1993.

American Psychiatric Association, DSM-5 Task Force. *Diagnostic and Statistical Manual (DSM-5)*, 5th ed. New York: American Psychiatric Association, 2013.

Bibi, Elizabeth. "Video and Photos: Vice President Kamala Harris, Actors Sheryl Lee Ralph, Abbi Jacobson and Chanté Adams Join Human Rights Campaign Incoming President Kelley Robinson at HRC Annual Dinner." Human Rights Campaign. October 30, 2022. https://www.hrc.org/press-releases/video-and-photos-vice-president-kamala-harris-actors-sheryl-lee-ralph-abbi-jacobson-and-chant%C3%A9-adams-join-human-rights-campaign-incoming-president-kelley-robinson-at-hrc-annual-dinner.

Delahooke, Mona. *Beyond Behaviors: Using Brain Science and Compassion to Understand and Solve Children's Behavioral Challenges*. Eau Claire, WI: PESI Publishing & Media, 2019.

Freyd, Jennifer. *Blind to Betrayal: Why We Fool Ourselves We Aren't Being Fooled*. New Jersey: Wiley, 2013.

Gottman, John M., and Nan Silver. *7 Principles for Making Marriage Work: A Practical Guide from the Country's Foremost Relationship Expert.* New York: Harmony Books, 2015.

Halchuk, Rebecca E., Judy A. Makinen, and Susan M. Johnson. "Resolving Attachment Injuries in Couples Using Emotionally Focused Therapy: A Three-Year Follow-Up." *Journal of Couple & Relationship Therapy* 9, no. 1 (2010): 31–47. https://doi.org/10.1080/15332690903473069.

Herman, Judith. *Trauma and Recovery.* New York: Basic Books, 2015.

Johnson, Sue and Brent Bradley. "Emotionally Focused Couple Therapy: Creating Loving Relationships." In *The Wiley-Blackwell Handbook of Family Psychology,* edited by James H. Bray and Mark Stanton. 402–415. Oxford: Blackwell Publishing, 2009. https://doi.org/10.1002/9781444310238.ch27.

Kanesarajah, Jeeva, Michael Waller, Wu Yi Zheng, and Annette J. Dobson. "Unit Cohesion, Traumatic Exposure and Mental Health of Military Personnel." *Occupational Medicine* 66, no. 4 (2016): 308–315. https://doi.org/10.1093/occmed/kqw009.

Kennedy, Becky. *Good Inside: A Guide to Becoming the Parent You Want to Be.* New York: Harper Collins Publishers, 2022.

McCluskey, Una, Derek Roger, and Poppy Nash. "A Preliminary Study of the Role of Attunement in Adult Psychotherapy." *Human Relations* 50, no. 10 (2016): 1261–1273. https://doi.org/10.1177/001872679705001004.

McCorry, Laurie Kelly. "Physiology of the Autonomic Nervous System." *American Journal of Pharmaceutical Education* 71, no. 4 (2007): 78. https://doi.org/10.5688/aj710478.

McEwon, Bruce S. "Stress, Adaptation, and Disease: Allostasis and Allostatic Load." *Annals of the New York*

Academy of Sciences 840, no. 1 (1998): 33–44. https://doi. org/10.1111/j.1749-6632.1998.tb09546.x.

Morey, Rajendra A., Joseph E. Dunsmoor, Courtney C. Haswell, Vanessa M. Brown, Ajay Vora, Jacob Weiner, Daniel Stjepanovic, H. Ryan Wagner III, VA Mid-Atlantic MIRECC Workgroup, and Kevin S. LaBar. "Fear Learning Circuitry is Biased Toward Generalization of Fear Associations in Posttraumatic Stress Disorder." *Translational Psychiatry* 5, no. e700 (2015): 1–10. https://doi.org/10.1038/tp.2015.196.

Norman, Luke, Natalia Lawrence, Andrew Iles, Abdelmalek Benattayallah, and Anke Karl. "Attachment-Security Priming Attenuates Amygdala Activation to Social and Linguistic Threat." *Social Cognitive and Affective Neuroscience* 10, no. 6 (2015): 832–839. https://doi.org/10.1093/scan/nsu127.

Ogden, Pat, Kekuni Minton, and Clare Pain. *Trauma and the Body: A Sensorimotor Approach to Psychotherapy.* New York: W. W. Norton & Company, 2006.

Ogden, Pat, and Mason A. Sommers. "Sensorimotor Psychotherapy Training for Mental Health Professionals, Level I: Trauma." Sensorimotor Psychotherapy Institute, Professional Training Program. Accessed February 12, 2020. https:// sensorimotorpsychotherapy.org/curriculum/trauma/.

Owca, Jakub. "The Association between a Psychotherapist's Theoretical Orientation and Perception of Complex Trauma and Repressed Anger in the Fawn Response." PhD diss., The Chicago School of Professional Psychology, 2020). https:// www.proquest.com/openview/83faad71347dae7bba4d3b130d0 83e88/1?pq-origsite=gscholar&cbl=18750&diss=y.

Perry, Bruce D. *The Boy Who Was Raised as a Dog.* New York: Basic Books, 2017.

Perry, Bruce D., and Oprah Winfrey. *What Happened to You?: Conversations on Trauma, Resilience, and Healing*. New York: Flatiron Books, 2021.

Poole-Heller, Diane. *The Power of Attachment: How to Create Deep and Lasting Intimate Relationships*. Boulder, CO: Sounds True, 2019.

Porges, Stephen W. "Polyvagal Theory: A Science of Safety." *Frontiers in Integrative Neuroscience* 16, no. 871227 (2022): 1–15. https://doi.org/10.3389/fnint.2022.871227.

Porges, Stephen W. *The Polyvagal Theory: Neurophysiological Foundations of Emotions, Attachment, Communication, and Self-regulation*. New York: W. W. Norton & Company, 2011.

Schwartz, Richard C. *No Bad Parts: Healing Trauma and Restoring Wholeness with the Internal Family Systems Mode*. Boulder, CO: Sounds True, 2021.

Schwartz, Richard C., and Martha Sweezy. *Internal Family Systems Therapy*. New York: The Guilford Press, 2020.

Siegel, Daniel J. *The Developing Mind: How Relationships and the Brain Interact to Shape Who We Are*, 2nd ed. New York: The Guilford Press, 2012.

Shin, Lisa M., Scott L. Rauch, and Roger K. Pitman. "Amygdala, Medial Prefrontal Cortex, and Hippocampal Function in PTSD." *Psychobiology of Posttraumatic Stress Disorder: A Decade of Progress* 1071, no. 1 (2006): 67–79. https://doi.org/10.1196/annals.1364.007.

Urban, Melissa. *The Book of Boundaries: Set the Limits That Will Set You Free*. New York: The Dial Press, 2022.

Van der Kolk, Bessal A. "Trauma and Memory." *Journal of Psychiatry and Clinical Neurosciences* 52, no. S1 (1998): S52–S64. https://doi.org/10.1046/j.1440-1819.1998.0520s5S97.x.

Walker, Pete. *Complex PTSD: From Surviving to Thriving: A Guide and Map for Recovering from* Childhood *Trauma*. Scotts Valley, CA: CreateSpace, 2014.

Wehrwein, Erica A., Hakan S. Orer, and Susan M. Barman. "Overview of the Anatomy, Physiology, and Pharmacology of the Autonomic Nervous System." *Comprehensive Physiology* 6, no. 3 (2016): 1239–1278. https://doi.org/10.1002/cphy.c150037.

Winnicott, Donald W. "The Theory of the Parent-Infant Relationship." *International Journal of Psychoanalysis* 41 (1960): 585–595. PMID: 13785877. https://tcf-website-media-library.s3.eu-west-2.amazonaws.com/wp-content/uploads/2021/09/21095241/Winnicott-D.-1960.-The-Theory-of-the-Parent-Infant-Relationship.-International-Journal-of-Psycho-Analysis.-411.-pp.585-595-1.pdf.

Word, Karen R., Suzanne H. Austin, and John C. Wingfield. "Allostasis Revisited: A Perception, Variation, and Risk Framework." *Frontiers in Ecology and Evolution* 10 (2022): 1–10. https://doi.org/10.3389/fevo.2022.954708.

Reader Resources

Websites

- Adult Survivors of Child Abuse (ASCA): www.ascasupport.org
- American Psychological Association's Psychologist Locator: https://locator.apa.org/
- Anxiety & Depression Association of America: www.adaa.org/netforum/findatherapist
- Bessel van der Kolk's Trauma Research Foundation: http://www.besselvanderkolk.com/
- Christine Courtois's trauma resources: http://drchriscourtois.com/home.html
- David Baldwin's Trauma Information Pages: www.trauma-pages.com/support.php
- EMDR Institute: https://www.emdr.com/
- IFS Institute: www.ifs-institute.com
- International Institute for Trauma & Addiction Professionals (IITAP): https://iitap.com/
- International Society for the Study of Trauma and Dissociation: www.isst-d.org/default
- International Society for Traumatic Stress Studies: https://istss.org/home

- Janina Fischer's TIST resources: https://janinafisher.com/tist
- MaleSurvivor: www.malesurvivor.org
- National Institute of Mental Health: www.nimh.nih.gov/index.shtml
- Psychology Self-Help Resources on the Internet: www.psychwww.com/resource/selfhelp.htm
- Recovery from Sexual Abuse's Blog Carnival: www.recovery-fromsexualabuse.blogspot.com
- Sidran Institute for Traumatic Stress Education & Advocacy: www.sidran.org

Hotlines and Phone Numbers

- Transgender Community
  - Trans Lifeline: 877-565-8860
- LGBTQ+ Youth
  - LGBT National Youth Talkline: 1-800-246-7743
  - The Trevor Project's Lifeline: 1-866-488-7386
  - The Trevor Project's Text Line: text START to 678-678
  - The Steve Fund Crisis Text Line: text STEVE to 741741
- LGBTQIA+ Adults
  - Lifeline: 1-800-273-8255
  - Crisis Text Line: text HOME to 741741
- All Ages
  - Gay, Lesbian, Bisexual and Transgender National Hotline: 1-888-843-4564
  - National Suicide Prevention Lifeline: 988 or 1-800-273-8255
- General Trauma
  - National Center for Victims of Crime: 1-800-FYI-CALL (394-2255)
  - National Child Abuse Hotline: 1-800-422-4453

- National Domestic Violence Hotline: 1-800-799-SAFE (7233)
- National Runaway Switchboard: 1-800-786-2929
- National Sexual Assault Hotline: 1-800-656-4673
- National Suicide Prevention Lifeline: 1-800-273-TALK (8255)
- National Teen Dating Abuse Helpline: 1-866-331-9474 or 1-866-331-8453

Books

- General Trauma
  - *Complex PTSD: From Surviving to Thriving* by Pete Walker
  - *Healing Trauma: Attachment, Mind, Body and Brain* (Norton Series on Interpersonal Neurobiology) by Daniel J. Siegel and Marion F. Solomon
  - *It's Not You, It's What Happened to You: Complex Trauma and Treatment* by Christine A. Courtois
  - *The Body Keeps the Score: Brain, Mind, and Body in the Healing of Trauma* by Bessel van der Kolk
  - *The Boy Who Was Raised as a Dog* by Bruce D. Perry
  - *The Healing Power of Emotion: Affective Neuroscience, Development & Clinical Practice* (Norton Series on Interpersonal Neurobiology) by Diana Fosha, Daniel J. Siegel, and Marion F. Soloman
  - *Trauma and Recovery: The Aftermath of Violence—from Domestic Abuse to Political Terror* by Judith Herman
  - *Treating Complex Traumatic Stress Disorders (Adults): Scientific Foundations and Therapeutic Models* by Christine A. Courtois and Julian Ford.

- Biology of Trauma
  - *Beyond Behaviors: Using Brain Science and Compassion to Understand and Solve Children's Behavioral Challenges* by Mona Delahooke
  - *Body Sense: The Science and Practice of Embodied Self-Awareness* (Norton Series on Interpersonal Neurobiology) by Alan Fogel
  - *It Didn't Start with You: How Inherited Family Trauma Shapes Who We Are and How to End the Cycle* by Mark Wolynn
  - *The Archaeology of Mind: Neuroanatomy Origins of Human Emotions* by Jaak Panksepp and Lucy Biven
  - *The Emotional Life of Your Brain: How Its Unique Patterns Affect the Way You Think, Feel, and Live—and How You Can Change Them* by Richard J. Davidson and Sharon Begley
  - *The Polyvagal Theory: Neurophysiological Foundations of Emotions, Attachment, Communication, and Self-Regulation* by Stephen W. Porges
- Body-Oriented/Somatic Approaches
  - *In an Unspoken Voice: How the Body Releases Trauma and Restores Goodness* by Peter A. Levine
  - *Nurturing Resilience: Helping Clients Move Forward from Developmental Trauma—An Integrative Somatic Approach* by Kathy L. Kain and Stephen J. Terrell
  - *The Neuroscience of Psychotherapy: Healing the Social Brain* (Norton Series on Interpersonal Neurobiology) by Louis Cozzolino
  - *Trauma and the Body: A Sensorimotor Approach to Psychotherapy* (Norton Series on Interpersonal Neurobiology) by Pat Ogden, Kekuni Minton, and Clare Pain
  - *Waking the Tiger: Healing Trauma* by Peter A. Levine

- EMDR
  - *Attachment-Focused EMDR: Healing Relational Trauma* by Laura Parnell
  - *EMDR: The Breakthrough Therapy for Overcoming Anxiety, Stress, and Trauma* by Francine Shapiro and Margot Silk Forrest
  - *Getting Past Your Past: Take Control of Your Life with Self-Help Techniques from EMDR Therapy* by Francine Shapiro
- Parts/Ego-States
  - *Easy Ego State Interventions: Strategies for Working with Parts* by Robin Shapiro
  - *Healing the Fragmented Selves of Trauma Survivors: Overcoming Internal Self-Alienation* by Janina Fisher
  - *Integrative Sex & Couples Therapy: A Therapist's Guide to New and Innovative Approaches* by Tammy Nelson
  - *Internal Family Systems Therapy* by Richard C. Schwartz and Martha Sweezy
  - *No Bad Parts: Healing Trauma and Restoring Wholeness with the Internal Family Systems Model* by Richard Schwartz
  - *Parts Work: An Illustrated Guide to Your Inner Life* by Tom Holmes
  - *The Haunted Self: Structural Dissociation and the Treatment of Chronic Traumatization* (Norton Series on Interpersonal Neurobiology) by Onno van der Hart, Ellert R. S. Nijenhuis, and Kathy Steele
  - *The Trauma Treatment Handbook: Protocols Across the Spectrum* by Robin Shapiro
- Couples/Relationships
  - *The Science of Trust: Emotional Attunement for Couples* by John M. Gottman

- *Intimacy From the Inside Out: Courage and Compassion in Couple Therapy* by Toni Herbine-Blank, Donna M. Kerpelman, and Martha Sweezy
- *More Than Words: The Science of Deepening Love and Connection in Any Relationship* by John Howard
- *The Practice of Emotionally Focused Couple Therapy: Creating Connection* by Susan M. Johnson
- *The Power of Attachment: How to Create Deep and Lasting Intimate Relationships* by Diane Poole Heller
- *Couples Therapy Workbook for Healing: Emotionally Focused Therapy Techniques to Restore Your Relationship* by Lori Cluff Schade

About the Author

Dr. Jen Towns is a trauma therapist, a social work professor, a queer woman, and a trauma survivor. She has worked in the social work field for over two decades—providing clinical treatment in a variety of settings and specializing in complex interpersonal trauma and relationships. Dr. Towns also teaches social work in higher education and has been a member of many workgroups that focus on advancing equality and social justice through education, therapy, and political action. She currently resides in Michigan with her wife, daughters, and two goldendoodles.

The B Corp Movement

Dear reader,

Thank you for reading this book and joining the Publish Your Purpose community! You are joining a special group of people who aim to make the world a better place.

What's Publish Your Purpose About?

Our mission is to elevate the voices often excluded from traditional publishing. We intentionally seek out authors and storytellers with diverse backgrounds, life experiences, and unique perspectives to publish books that will make an impact in the world.

Certified

Beyond our books, we are focused on tangible, action-based change. As a woman- and LGBTQ+-owned company, we are committed to reducing inequality, lowering levels of poverty, creating a healthier environment, building stronger communities, and creating high-quality jobs with dignity and purpose.

(B)

®

Corporation

As a Certified B Corporation, we use business as a force for good. We join a community of mission-driven companies building a more equitable, inclusive, and sustainable global economy. B Corporations must meet high standards of transparency, social and environmental performance, and accountability as determined by the nonprofit B Lab. The certification process is rigorous and ongoing (with a recertification requirement every three years).

How Do We Do This?

We intentionally partner with socially and economically disadvantaged businesses that meet our sustainability goals. We embrace and encourage our authors and employee's differences in race, age, color, disability, ethnicity, family or marital status, gender identity or expression, language, national origin, physical and mental ability, political affiliation, religion, sexual orientation, socio-economic status, veteran status, and other characteristics that make them unique.

Community is at the heart of everything we do—from our writing and publishing programs to contributing to social enterprise nonprofits like reSET (https://www.resetco.org/) and our work in founding B Local Connecticut.

We are endlessly grateful to our authors, readers, and local community for being the driving force behind the equitable and sustainable world we are building together.

To connect with us online, or publish with us, visit us at www.publishyourpurpose.com.

Elevating Your Voice,

Jenn T Grace

Jenn T. Grace
Founder, Publish Your Purpose

.